Historic Rural Churches of Georgia

HISTORIC RURAL CHURCHES of GEORGIA

Sonny Seals and George S. Hart

PUBLISHED IN ASSOCIATION WITH GEORGIA HUMANITIES

The University of Georgia Press   Athens

A Wormsloe
FOUNDATION
PUBLICATION

All historical maps are courtesy of the Hargrett Rare Books
and Manuscript Library / University of Georgia Libraries

Published by the University of Georgia Press
Athens, Georgia 30602
www.ugapress.org
Designed by Erin Kirk New
Set in Centaur
Printed and bound by Pacom
The paper in this book meets the guidelines for
permanence and durability of the Committee on
Production Guidelines for Book Longevity of the
Council on Library Resources.

Most University of Georgia Press titles are
available from popular e-book vendors.

Printed in Korea
20   19   18   c   5   4   3   2

Library of Congress Cataloging-in-Publication Data
Names: Seals, Sonny, 1942– author. | Hart, George, 1942– author.
Title: Historic rural churches of Georgia / Sonny Seals and George S. Hart.
Description: Athens : University of Georgia Press in association with
    Georgia Humanities, [2016] | Includes bibliographical references.
Identifiers: LCCN 2015037378 | ISBN 9780820349350 (hardcover : alk. paper)
Subjects: LCSH: Church buildings—Georgia. | Historic buildings—Georgia. |
    Rural churches—Georgia. | Georgia—Church history.
Classification: LCC NA5230.G4 S43 2016 | DDC 726.509758—dc23 LC record available
    at http://lccn.loc.gov/2015037378

Publication of this book was supported
in part by the Montgomery Foundation,
the Kenneth Coleman Series in Georgia History
and Culture, Rick and Linda Allen,
and Candy Gilliland.

This book is dedicated to our talented group of volunteer photographers, whose evocative and important work can also be seen at our Historic Rural Churches of Georgia website, www.hrcga.org. Their passion and respect for Georgia's rural history lives on in print in this volume. This book is also dedicated to our lovely and forbearing wives, who have allowed us free rein to pursue our passion for telling Georgia's history through the eyes of her rural churches.

Contents

Foreword   JIMMY CARTER

When Rosalynn and I grew up in rural Georgia, the church served as the center of our lives. I believe this was true for nearly all others in our region. Those of us who lived in or near Plains, in Sumter County, worshipped, studied, and celebrated at Baptist, Methodist, and Lutheran churches. Two of these churches, St. Mark's Lutheran Church and Plains Baptist Church, are included in this handsome and important book.

Rosalynn's great-grandparents, George Calhoun Wise and Francis Elizabeth Coogle, were Lutherans whose ancestors had fled religious persecution in eighteenth-century Germany and settled in South Carolina. After the Civil War, in which George Calhoun lost a leg, he and many of his family and friends moved from South Carolina to our region in Georgia. In 1870, he was a founder and builder of St. Mark's Lutheran Church. He is said to have planed the rough-cut lumber for the structure.

This church remained part of Rosalynn's family life. The land on which it was built now belongs to us. The church was active when we were children, and even after it stopped holding regular services it was the site of annual homecoming celebrations. The cemetery remains where it always was, but the church building has been moved and beautifully restored.

Rosalynn was not raised a Lutheran, however. Her grandmother had married John William Murray, who was a Baptist, and their daughter, Allie, had married Wilburn Edgar Smith, a Methodist. The Smiths raised their daughter Rosalynn as a Methodist, but she regularly attended all three churches. She became a Baptist after our marriage.

I grew up at the Plains Baptist Church. It was founded as the Lebanon Baptist Church in 1848, and the first church building was erected where the Lebanon Baptist Cemetery, 1½ miles west of Plains, is today. My father, mother, and other members of my family are buried there. The current structure was completed within the city limits of Plains in 1906, and the church was later renamed Plains Baptist Church. After returning home from Washington, Rosalynn and I transferred our memberships to the Maranatha Baptist Church, but the old Plains church edifice is still very meaningful to us.

As a boy, I also attended the Methodist church, because the Baptists and Methodists alternated Sunday services. We also would attend other churches when revivals were being held. While there are theological differences among denominations, we did not pay much attention to them at the time.

In the racially segregated society of my childhood, white people and black people belonged to different churches, but on occasion my family and I would visit St. Mark African Methodist Episcopal Church, located close to our farm in Archery. This usually was when Bishop William Decker Johnson was preaching. He was the most prominent man in our community, with religious responsibilities over AME churches in several states. The emotional spirit of the services at St. Mark far exceeded anything we experienced at our regular church.

The largest congregation in the Plains area is another African American church, the Lebanon Baptist Church. Earlier, a church of the same name had served both blacks and whites, but after the War between the States the membership split and the black church retained the name, while the white church became the Plains Baptist Church.

To understand the history of Georgia, it is essential to understand the role that religion played in the lives of the people. Unlike some of the other original thirteen colonies, Georgia was not founded for religious purposes, but as the settlers created communities they also created churches. In rural Georgia, these and the schools often were the only public buildings outside the county seats, and most Georgians lived in rural communities up until the 1950s. The purpose of *Historic Rural Churches of Georgia* is not only to present the stories of rural churches, but also to preserve them. The excellent photographs of the book contribute to this, but we hope that these will inspire people throughout the state to preserve the physical structures, as well.

I am pleased that the book honors churches of both black and white communities. The heritage of slavery and segregation does not arouse pride, but we *can* be proud of the churches created by African Americans, and I hope that this book gives special encouragement to their preservation. I am proud to be associated with the book and the movement to preserve the historic rural churches of Georgia.

Preface

I met my lifelong friend, George Hart, in 1960. I was a student at Georgia Tech, and George was a musical prodigy and a student at Emory. Over the years, he has given me many gifts. One of these is a passion for bluegrass music and another is a love of the Georgia backroads and the history that goes with it. George and I have been periodically riding the back roads of Georgia for years, with no other motivation than the sheer joy of discovery. Just jostling along those lonely byways to see what was around the next curve was exciting in a strange and exotic sort of way . . . old towns that have virtually disappeared, farmhouses that are falling down, cemeteries covered in weeds, the decay of an agrarian way of life that seems so distant and yet so near. We thought at some point we would get it out of our system, but the more we learned about Georgia's unique beginnings, the more fascinating it became.

On one of our backroads sojourns, we went through the village of Powelton in Hancock County between Crawfordville and Sparta. Powelton was in a very remote location but one could tell that it had once been a thriving community. There was a main-street kind of feel to it, with a single road running the length of the old town, but now there were just a few old houses with kudzu running through the windows and a little store that had been closed for decades. Other than this, the only significant structures remaining were a Baptist church at one end of town and a Methodist church at the other end, only a few hundred yards apart. The historical marker outside the Baptist church noted that the church was organized in 1786 and that Jesse Mercer,

Depressions and fieldstones mark the earliest graves in the cemetery at the old Powelton Methodist Church.

one of the pillar founders of the Baptist Church in Georgia, used to preach there. Obviously, this had been an important village over two hundred years ago.

The old Methodist church at the other end of town was embraced by a small, very old graveyard where depressions and fieldstones marked the earliest graves. There were later graves where collapsing false crypts and weathered headstones of many styles stood. I spotted a Confederate headstone on the edge of the woods and walked over to read it: "Sergeant William D. Seals—4th Sgt—Co. K—15th Ga Inf." I had visited many old cemeteries in our back roads travels but had found very few markers inscribed with the surname Seals. Could this be a relative of mine in this remote site? As I found out later, this casual but fateful encounter had been with my great-grandfather. I knew I had been born in Augusta, but otherwise my family history was a mystery to me. On the other hand, George's family had a long and storied history beginning in Greene County, just up the road.

The blank wall that had been obscuring my family history was about to come tumbling down. Beginning with this headstone, I used the power of the internet to uncover the story of my family roots. My Seals family had arrived in Virginia from England in the mid-1600s, migrated into North Carolina, and around 1785 landed in what soon would be named Hancock County. My forebearers, like their fellow settlers, were hardworking farmers proud to own a few acres of their own and were willing to carve out a life on the Georgia frontier.

The Civil War chapter of the family history was heartrending. The Fifteenth Georgia Infantry, William D. Seals's unit, participated in some of the worst of that bloody war—Seven Days, Antietam, Gettysburg, Chickamauga, the Wilderness, and more. Wounded in the Battle of the Wilderness, Sergeant Seals had lost a brother at Antietam, and would soon lose another in the Battle of Jonesboro. He came home at the age of twenty four, married, and fathered eleven children. In 1904 he would apply for an Indigent Confederate Pension, stating that he had no assets, no income, and depended on the charity of his children. This sad story was not unusual—it happened all over the South. Learning how my family had suffered so helped me understand and appreciate on a deeper level the enormous sacrifice of everyone involved.

Given these insights, George and I wanted to understand more about what happened in this part of Georgia before and after that war. We wondered about the lost village of Powelton. Why was it there and why did it disappear? We were just as curious to learn more about the beautiful but deserted Methodist church. Who owned it now? Who was taking care of it? What was going to happen to it? How could we, as a civilized society, let an historic and beautiful sanctuary like this collapse and disappear? The answers to questions like these formed the cornerstone of our early plans for *Historic Rural Churches of Georgia*.

The long-abandoned Cedar Grove Methodist Church in Tattnall County (shown here) illustrates a sad fate for small rural churches. As a once-vibrant rural community is slowly decimated by death and by migration to more urban locales, the church falls into disrepair and finally to ruin. Since these old "box" churches were often built using local materials and simple construction techniques, basic repairs needn't be expensive, and people are often generous about donating labor and materials. Indeed, only three ingredients are necessary to save these structures: a group of local

people willing to raise funds and oversee the project, a bit of repair money, and an ongoing use for the church to ensure its future maintenance.

After much discussion and thought, we resolved to make people more aware of the problem of disintegrating churches and disappearing history. By increasing awareness, we hoped to facilitate preservation efforts that might not come about otherwise. Our first big effort was to establish a website (www.hrcga.org) that would attract the attention of other interested individuals. We wanted to make these old sanctuaries come alive with beautiful photographs, while paying appropriate attention to the primitive architectural beauty of the structures. We also wanted to tell some of the stories of the rural pioneers who founded and built these treasures. The surrounding burial grounds would yield their own "tales from the crypt" within this historical perspective, so we appropriately devote attention to them.

Cedar Grove Methodist in Tattnall County was built in 1887. It has been abandoned for decades, but with some local leadership, it can still be saved.

We are deeply indebted to the cadre of volunteer photographers who helped us develop our "reverential documentation" style of photography. We are equally indebted to countless others who donated time and services, as well as the hundreds of citizens throughout Georgia who directed us to the churches they loved and gave us their time, photographs, and memories. The positive responses we received to our website and to our Facebook page led to this book.

The churches featured in these pages represent some of the most interesting historic churches around the state. We have documented many more, but space limitations permit only a limited number here. We have chosen an eclectic group, spread throughout the state, that we feel will be of interest to all. Each entry lists the name of the church, its county location, and the date the church was organized. Each caption is intended to help bring the photograph to life for the reader.

Most churches followed a traditional progression from brush arbor to log cabin to one or more frame structures. Construction dates of the present structure are given in the entry when they are known or can be ascertained, but of course such records have not always survived. Our selection criteria are subjective, but we value interesting historical background, rural locations, architectural eye appeal, and older cemeteries. The current structure needs to be a minimum of a hundred years old. Each entry is worthy for a different reason—sometimes the story is the church itself, sometimes it is the location, and sometimes it resides in the cemetery.

Our research into these church stories began to lead us on a different sort of journey through early Georgia history, and historical maps help us visualize that journey. In 1732, the territory between the British Crown land in South Carolina and the Spanish land of Florida was unoccupied by any European power. The land that we now know as Georgia consisted of well over 30 million acres. This Debatable Land, as it was known then, was the traditional hunting grounds for two major tribes—the Creeks to the

south and west and the Cherokees to the north. Georgia, when founded in 1733 under the leadership of Parliament member James Oglethorpe, served as a military buffer for the crown lands in South Carolina against Spanish encroachment from the south. When the framers signed the Declaration of Independence in 1776, the new state of Georgia was inhabited by an estimated 25,000 whites and 14,500 blacks, residing mostly along the lower Savannah River and the coastal Low Country.

The Treaty of Paris in 1783 ended hostilities with the British and set the southern boundary of Georgia, as well as the southern border of our new nation. At the end of the conflict, most of Georgia still belonged to Native Americans. As the white population of the state grew, the federal government steadily acquired, through a series of treaties with the Creeks and the Cherokees, extensive parcels of land from one river basin to the next. These tracts were then opened for white settlement, which was the key to Georgia's rapid expansion. The area of white settlement advanced relentlessly from the Oconee River to the Ocmulgee, to the Flint, and finally to the Chattahoochee.

This insatiable appetite for land on the part of the Europeans and their descendants fueled land acquisitions for half a century of treaties and seizures. The discovery of gold in North Georgia was another factor, ultimately resulting in the expulsion of the Cherokees and the infamous Trail of Tears. The last of the Creek lands were ceded by 1827. The Cherokees resisted, successfully challenging the government of Georgia in the U.S. Supreme Court. However, a corrupt faction of the Cherokees was thereafter bribed into signing another treaty. By 1839, the last of the Cherokees had been removed by the U.S. Army, resulting in the state's current footprint. The 1840 census counted in Georgia 410,448 free citizens and 280,944 slaves in ninety-three counties.

The distribution of this land was another key element in Georgia's evolution. Each treaty yielded vast acreage that had to be organized in some fashion and placed in private hands.

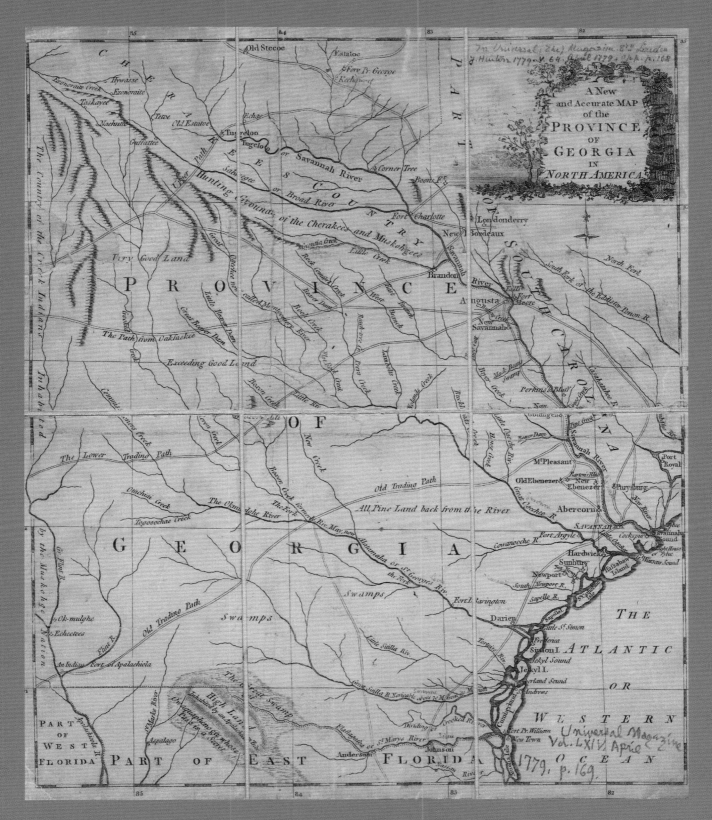

This British map from 1779 shows the "Province of Georgia" to be limited to a very few towns along the coast, such as Darien, Sunbury, and Savannah. The only other towns were located along the Savannah River from the coast on the south to Augusta on the north. Note the references on the map to various features such as the "Hunting ground of the Cherakees and Muskohgees," "Very Good Land," and "Exceeding Good Land." Rebel residents of Georgia, of course, would have considered themselves a state rather than a province of the Crown in 1779.

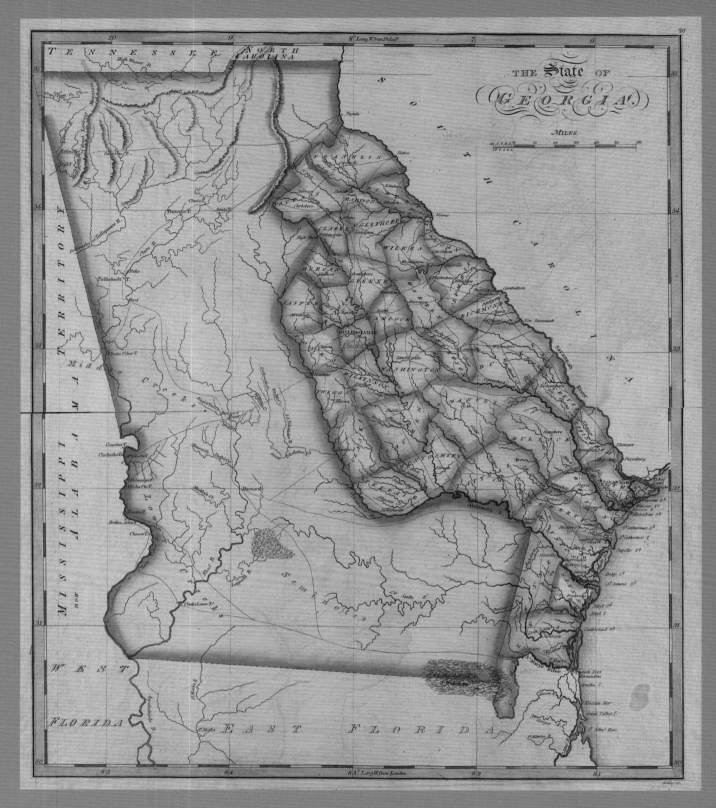

The federal government set the boundaries of Georgia in 1802, but most of the land within its borders
still belonged to the Indians. By 1813, Georgia consisted of thirty-nine counties and its western frontier
had expanded through various Indian treaties, first to the Ogeechee River, then to the Oconee, and
finally to the Ocmulgee. The western edge of the frontier now included the towns of Madison,
Monticello, Clinton, and Hawkinsville.

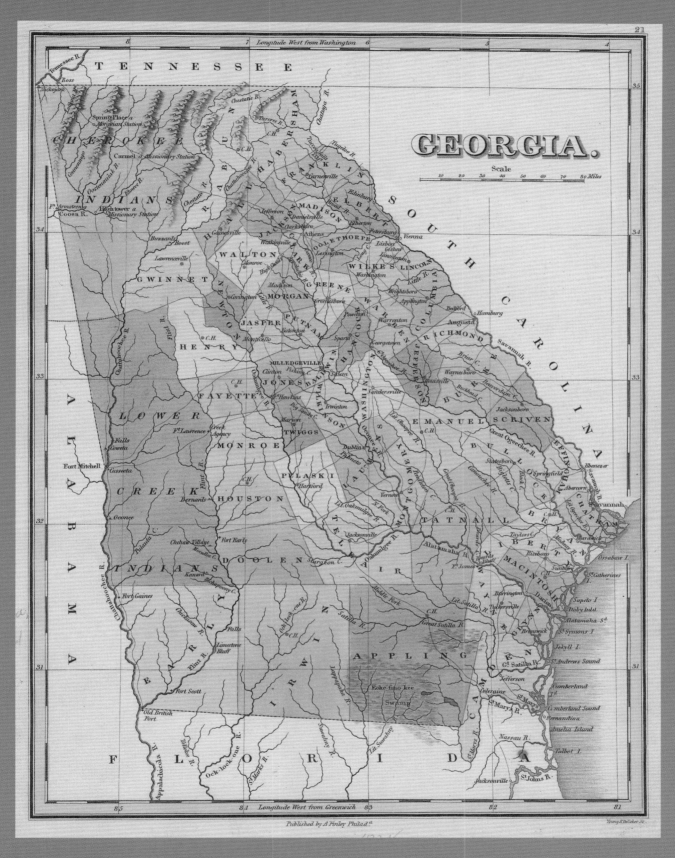

GEORGIA.

Scale
10 20 30 40 50 60 70 80 Miles

Published by A Finley Philad.ᵃ   Young & Delleker Sc.

By 1824, the western frontier had expanded to the Flint River. Georgia land still under Creek control was limited to that between the Flint and the Chattahoochee. Cherokee holdings had been reduced to the northwestern corner of the state, north of the Chattahoochee.

By 1831, the western border had become the Chattahoochee River and all Creek lands had disappeared. Cherokee holdings had been reduced further in the northwest corner, and the Indian Removal Act of 1830 had set the stage for the final chapter. After 1832 Georgia's possession of all lands within its boundaries was complete. At the end of that year, there were eighty-nine counties.

The state developed both a "headright" system of distribution and a lottery system to allow the new land to be parceled out to land-hungry pioneers in small plots, giving preference to Revolutionary War veterans. The majority of the distributions consisted of 200 acres or less. The Georgia lottery system conducted eight land lotteries from 1805 to 1833. Georgia's story is one of virtually free land open to any white man tough enough and willing to work it.

Apart from the residents of Savannah and Augusta, the inhabitants of Georgia had participated in very little religion of any sort until after the Revolution. Few early Georgians had embraced the Church of England, and after the Revolution few had an affinity for any form of religion with ties to Europe or hierarchical structure. What changed this was the Great Awakening, a movement that swept the U.S. South, including Georgia, between 1790 and 1830, bringing a more democratic form of Christianity modeled after the Christian communities of the New Testament.

This blossoming of religious fervor is explained in detail in the introduction by Professor Tom Scott that follows. First the Baptists, and then the Methodists, won the hearts and minds of the early Georgia pioneers as these two denominations came to dominate the rural countryside. The histories of the older churches reveal that, in the rapidly emerging backcountry, the churches were the center of everything. They were the first institutions to be established—the towns, the county court systems, and everything else followed. In the absence of other civil and municipal institutions, churches provided spiritual comfort, social structure, unity, and basic law and order in an immense wilderness populated by a diverse group of rugged, small landowners.

Early church minutes reveal the unmistakably powerful role of the churches as, first the community building blocks from which our state emerged, and then the social glue that held it together. The churches performed as community center, dating service, courthouse (complete with judge and jury), and everything else these individualistic settlers needed in order to function as a civilized society. After a peer review of the transgression, the ultimate punishment in the backcountry for unacceptable social behavior was excommunication.

Later developments in Georgia's evolution to the present would include the swift rise of King Cotton, the consolidation of landowners, and the resulting dramatic increase in slavery. The rural churches practiced antebellum religious segregation. In the first half of the nineteenth century, this practice was an early demonstration of cultural divisions that would lead to political stresses developing throughout Georgia and other southern states. Both the Baptists and the Methodists developed serious internal differences regarding slavery, separating into northern and southern factions as a result. The churches and the cemeteries also reveal the heavy burden borne by many Georgia families as the Civil War swept the state.

Through rural churches, we learn about Georgia's race relations in an antebellum and then postbellum world. As the state slowly rose from the ashes, churches were the major source of spiritual healing for both whites and blacks, although in different ways. At the end of the nineteenth century, churches continued to play a prominent role in shaping the culture and future of the state's citizens. That future would include embracing universal public education, the rise of industrialism, and the ultimate diminution of the rural, agrarian lifestyle that had been Georgia's foundation.

These historic rural churches of Georgia are a vital part of who we are and how we got here. Most of them are still there, on lonely backroads or in rural villages—some of which have virtually disappeared. They should be treasured and preserved for future generations, and it is our hope that this book will help accomplish that worthwhile mission.

SONNY SEALS AND GEORGE HART

Introduction   Religion in Georgia   JOHN THOMAS SCOTT

Churches connect the divine with the human, values with social forms, and aspiration with present reality.
At once messengers and agents, mirrors and actors, they enable people to think through their ideas about
religiosity and convey them to the rest of the world while, in turn, influencing those ideas and shaping religion
and society. Within church spaces, God, clergy, and laity meet and negotiate their respective relationships.
—Jeanne Halgren Kilde, *When Church Became Theatre*

Church building did not begin in Georgia, but building churches occupied the
founders' intentions even before James Oglethorpe set foot on the Yamacraw
Bluff in the late winter of 1733. Having worshipped in houses and caves during
Christianity's first several centuries, Christians began building separate houses
of worship—churches—sometime in the third century after Christ. Following a
variety of architectural patterns over the centuries—some dictated by theology,
some by technology and local materials—Christians built churches large and
small, simple and elaborate, as the religion spread from the Levant to Europe
and eventually the world. Indeed, church building became among the most
common activity of believers of every stripe—Coptic, Catholic, Orthodox, and
Protestant—and one of the most common activities of European colonists of
every empire founded in the New World—Spanish, French, Portuguese, Dutch,
and English. In the area that eventually became Georgia, the Spanish had built
Roman Catholic churches along the coast in the seventeenth century, whereas
English colonists had built Puritan churches in New England, Anglican churches in
Virginia and elsewhere, and Quaker meetinghouses in Pennsylvania.[1] Church

building represented the planting of Christianity in the area, and the founders of Georgia, collectively known as the Trustees, considered planting Christianity not just a requisite but an integral part of their venture. As it turned out, the colony did not develop religiously as the Trustees had planned; they had hoped for a mostly Anglican colony that would allow "dissenters" (Roman Catholics excepted) to worship in peace. The charter itself specifically held that "there shall be a liberty of conscience allowed in the worship of God, to all persons inhabiting [Georgia], and that all such persons (except papists) shall have a free exercise of religion."[2] Over the next century, however, as the colony moved through royal, revolutionary, republican, frontier, cotton kingdom, and postslavery phases, a multiplicity of Christian groups—some old, some new—occupied the growing territory of Georgia and established themselves and their church buildings across the state. Owing to the largely rural nature of Georgia's society and economy well into the twentieth century, most of these groups centered their efforts on locales far from the relatively few cities in Georgia. The buildings and cemeteries they built testify both to the importance of religion in the lives of many settlers—black and white, slave and free—and to the rural life ways they experienced.

The Trustees who founded Georgia in the early 1730s intended and expected Anglicanism to be the primary religious expression of the colony but intentionally allowed for and even recruited some dissenting groups to the colony. Anglicanism, formed out of the tumult resulting from Henry VIII's efforts to obtain a male heir in the 1530s, had become a bulwark of Protestantism later in the century under his daughter Elizabeth, but the English church never became completely unified across British domains. Puritans, Brownists, Independents, Presbyterians, and eventually Quakers had all challenged the practices and governance of the Church of England in the seventeenth century, and most, by the end, had secured some measure of tolerance, though not official acceptance, from that body. Many of these groups had opted to take their dissent to the New World, establishing or being party to establishing colonies all along the Atlantic Seaboard. Puritans of one stripe or another had founded most of New England in the early seventeenth century; Quakers under the leadership of William Penn laid claim to much of the Middle Atlantic region; and by the middle of the eighteenth century Scots-Irish Presbyterians had flooded the colonies from New York to the Carolinas and occupied much of the backcountry. Still, many Anglicans hoped for a strong Anglican presence in the British Empire in the eighteenth century. One such individual, Thomas Bray, helped found two organizations—the Society for the Propagation of the Gospel in Foreign Parts (SPG) and the Society for the Propagation of Christian Knowledge (SPCK)—and gathered a group of friends around these organizations who proved pivotal to the founding and shaping of Georgia. Most of the Trustees affiliated directly with the SPG, the SPCK, or another group known as Bray's Associates, and all three groups and the Anglican Bishop of London (who after 1728 officially oversaw Anglican efforts in the New World) worked closely with the Trustees to ensure the planting of Christianity in general and Anglicanism in particular in the new colony.[3]

The Trustee period of colonial Georgia, which lasted about twenty years, proved largely unkind to Anglican efforts but saw the establishment of a variety of dissenting groups in the colony. Simply put, the Trustees and their affiliated groups had difficulty sending and keeping Anglican priests in the colony and as much difficulty building an infrastructure for Anglican churches and ministers to prosper there. Despite funding from many donors across England, the efforts rarely panned out. Those ministers who did come found it impossible to minister to the colonists and proselytize the Indians at the same time—too many people and too much territory combined with unforeseen developments hampered their efforts. The first minister, Henry Herbert, who arrived with Oglethorpe on the *Anne* in 1733, stayed only a short while and died on the voyage home. Samuel Quincy, his successor, remained at his post a bit longer, but by late 1735 Georgia found itself without a full-time Anglican priest. Oglethorpe, back in England in 1735, recruited the largest minister-missionary troupe of the Trustee era, consisting of three priests and a layman—John Wesley, Charles Wesley, Benjamin Ingham, and Charles Delamotte. The Wesleys ran into trouble with Oglethorpe and some of the settlers, and Ingham departed after a year. Only Delamotte remained by December 1737, but in the summer of 1738 he also left.[4] Their successors—William Norris and George Whitefield—remained only briefly as parish priests, clashed repeatedly with each other, and took different paths out of the colony. Accused of impregnating his German maid, Norris returned to England under a cloud, while Whitefield soon embarked on building Bethesda orphanage near Savannah and on transatlantic preaching tours that elevated him to heights of fame and popularity that the small Georgia colony could not offer. After a few other failed efforts, finally in the mid-1740s the Trustees found in Bartholomew Zouberbuhler a pastor for the Savannah church. In his two decades in Georgia, he brought stability to the Anglican presence in Georgia and in 1750 oversaw the construction of the first permanent Anglican church building in Savannah, Christ Church.[5] During the royal period (1752–1776), Anglicanism made only marginal progress within the colony owing to its elitist air and an "adversarial relationship" with the common folk. While it became the established church in the royal period and remained the denominational choice of Georgia elites, its footprint among the settlers of Georgia always remained relatively small.[6]

Nevertheless, the Trustee opening for other Christian groups to enter Georgia allowed for other denominations to establish themselves and their churches in the colony. Lutherans, known more popularly in Georgia history as the Salzburgers, established the Ebenezer settlement just north of Savannah along the river. These Protestant coreligionists had been chased from their Catholic lands and found sympathy from the Hanoverian British monarchy of the early 1730s. The SPCK in particular played a lead role in seeing a group of them settled in Georgia.[7] Moravians, another German group, undertook a number of foreign missionary enterprises in the early 1730s, and for a brief time in that decade played an important role in the life of Savannah before joining the Moravians already in Pennsylvania.[8] Needing fighting men to defend the colony from Spanish Florida, the Trustees invited a group of Scottish Highlanders to the colony in the mid-1730s. They founded the settlement of Darien and brought Presbyterianism to the state.[9] Congregationalists, the heirs of the seventeenth-century Puritan tradition, founded the town of Midway and the important port of Sunbury in the 1750s. Quakers founded Wrightsborough in the 1760s, but more importantly for later Georgia history, Baptists founded churches in the frontier region north of Augusta under the leadership of Daniel Marshall, who inspired a generation of Georgia Baptists to found churches over the next several decades.[10] Two important groups of non-Christians also entered Georgia in the colonial period. Several groups of Jewish settlers entered Savannah in the 1730s and formed the Mickve Israel congregation, although they built no synagogue until the early nineteenth century.[11] Slave merchants forcefully brought thousands of Africans to Georgia as slaves once slavery became legal at the end of the Trustee period, but the slaves had "relatively little to do with Christianity" in the colonial period and instead "remained devoted to the indigenous religions they had known."[12]

Although not an overly religious colony, among the other British American colonies it had a relatively diverse collection of religious groups. Most Georgians throughout the Trustee and the royal periods seemed to have at best limited interest in religion. One estimate places congregational membership in Georgia at less than 10 percent in the Revolutionary era, about half the colonial average.[13] Georgia's founding by Anglican churchmen, its elitist orientation, and its subsequent association directly with the crown of England (also the head of the Church of England) as a royal colony put Anglicanism in Georgia in a difficult position in the Revolutionary era. Its open charter

The oldest church structure in Georgia is Jerusalem Lutheran, Effingham County, built in 1768.

and its participation in the increasingly tolerant and pluralistic Protestant British culture of the eighteenth century, however, had created the opening necessary for numerous other groups to establish both congregations and churches in the colony by the time of the American Revolution.

Although many Christian ministers supported first the resistance movement and then the Revolution and later played important roles in the founding of the state and the new nation, Georgia did not experience significant religious numerical growth in the founding era. Christians of various sorts spread out across Georgia as it expanded in the decades before and after 1800, but in terms of raw numbers they remained a relatively small group within the state in the early national period. Some of the denominations suffered from revolutionary dislocation. As a consequence

of their association with the crown, Anglicans fell into disrepute in the republican revolutionary era and only slowly reconstituted themselves as Episcopalians in the new republic. Methodism, another offshoot of Anglicanism formed only in the 1780s, found difficult footing in Georgia as a result of the Wesleys' opposition to slavery and its having to create an ecclesiastical infrastructure from scratch. Presbyterians suffered from the defection of one of their most prominent Georgian ministers, John Joachim Zubly of Savannah, who had initially been a strong proponent of resistance to British measures in the early 1770s but ultimately found himself unable to back independence and revolution.[14] A newer, more skeptical approach to religion known broadly as Deism—an approach that attracted the likes of important national figures such as Thomas Paine,

Powelton Baptist, Hancock County, is the oldest Baptist sanctuary in the state, built in 1798.

Thomas Jefferson, and Benjamin Franklin—attracted some Georgians, as well. Elihu Palmer, a Presbyterian minister turned Deist, moved to Augusta in 1790 and opened the Richmond Academy, where he taught for a year and lectured publicly, finding Augusta "open to public discussion on subjects deemed unacceptable elsewhere." Georgia Senator James Jackson invited Denis Driscol, a nationally known newspaperman with Deist views, to Augusta in 1807 to run a Republican paper.[15] The state and nation's new commitment to the separation of church and state power eliminated the possibility of governmental support for religion in Georgia, and the rapid expansion of Georgia settlement in the decades following the revolution further stunted religious growth. With settlers spreading out from the Savannah to the Chattahoochee River by the 1820s,

Georgia religious groups were often unable to provide ministers or missionaries to these frontier folks and found life on the frontier too diffuse and disparate to create much of an ecclesiastical presence in the Federalist and Jeffersonian eras. Ecclesiastical and religious developments originating around 1800 eventually solved these problems for Georgia's religious groups—at least some of them—but in 1800 Georgia remained a relatively secular state.

By the middle of the nineteenth century Georgia had transformed from a relatively secular state into the buckle of the Bible Belt that stretched from Virginia across to Texas. As an important southern component to the larger U.S. evangelical empire of the nineteenth century, Georgia in its culture and demography grew more Christian and increasingly linked that Christianity to its politics, its economy, and its race relations. Those denominations that most closely identified with U.S. evangelicalism and its practices—primarily the Baptists and Methodists—grew exponentially in the nineteenth century, while the denominations that hesitated—primarily the Presbyterians and the Episcopalians—fell far behind. Importantly, evangelicalism also created an opening for conversions within the African slave community in numbers unseen in the colonial period—leading to the participation (albeit subserviently) of black slaves in white churches and the establishment of separate black churches and ministers in some locations. This expansion into the black community in the antebellum era paved the way for new black denominations and church buildings in the postbellum era. By the end of the nineteenth century, being a Christian in Georgia—white or black—had become almost synonymous with being an evangelical. This reality especially held true in rural areas, where country ways fit well with evangelical impulses.

Evangelicalism, which has grown up alongside modernity and still remains a significant religious force in early twenty-first-century America, arose as a transatlantic movement across denominational lines in the middle of the eighteenth century.[16] George Whitefield, the Wesleys, and Ingham—all of whom had come to Georgia in the 1730s—played central roles in the rise of British and U.S. evangelicalism in their post-Georgia lives. Centered on religious experience rather than intellectual assent or formal liturgy or ritual, evangelicalism emphasized "the call for a turning from the old self and world, in a conversion through an intense experience of Jesus Christ by the power of the Holy Spirit." That conversion experience combined with a "fresh resort to biblical authority supported by high claims for the literal accuracy of the Bible." These convictions then produced an effort at "ordered moral behavior," "efforts to witness and to share the faith," and participation in a local body of believers—a church.[17] In the eighteenth century, Presbyterians and Wesleyan Anglicans led the way, but by the turn of the nineteenth century Baptists and the newly formed Methodist church most closely

embraced the revivalistic practices of U.S. evangelicals. New denominations also emerged during the Great Revival, or Second Great Awakening, that swept through the South in the early nineteenth century, most notably for Georgia the Disciples of Christ (the Christian Church). As evangelicalism penetrated the slave and free-black communities in the antebellum era, black preachers emerged and black congregations formed across Georgia. Indeed, evangelicalism overturned in a few decades a century of Anglican and Presbyterian frustration with slave missions and equal frustration with a largely "lost" white population.

The Great Revival, as it became known, brought evangelicalism to the South and thus stands as a "watershed in the religious history of the South."[18] The revival centered for decades on the camp meeting—a rural, multiday, multidenominational religious event aimed at the "bringing on of conversions among those in attendance."[19] Importantly, though, while these camp meetings produced many of the converts, they also pushed them into new or existing denominations and church buildings to live out their Christian lives and "learn the language of Canaan," which was a "metaphor evoking the new awareness into which believers were initiated by undergoing repentance and rebirth"—a spiritual entry into the "Promised Land."[20] Camp meetings typically took place in rural settings over three or four days and involved ministers and lay leaders from multiple denominations. Bible reading, preaching, and singing—all aimed at convicting listeners of their sin and convincing them of the need for conversion—combined with often ecstatic physical reactions (called religious exercises) to produce converts by the tens of thousands across Georgia and the rest of the South.[21] Baptists, who had less stringent requirements for individuals to become ministers, and Methodists, who combined the camp meeting with the circuit rider to extend their ministerial reach, "benefited most from the Great Revival in Georgia." Although they had been at the forefront of the movement in the eighteenth and early nineteenth centuries, for theological and educational reasons Presbyterians eventually shied away from the more

Fountain Campground
was organized in 1822
and is still going strong
today.

expressive forms of evangelicalism and so lost in relative numbers to the Baptists and Methodists. Episcopalians, as a result of their Anglican roots, tended to favor liturgy and ritual over open expression and so likewise found themselves falling behind numerically, especially in rural areas.[22]

These early evangelicals "modeled their churches on the primitive Christian communities of the New Testament, fellowships knit together by emotional intimacy, and spiritual equality, godly discipline and self abasement."[23] Evangelicalism appealed to rural folk early on because of its straightforward message, its relatively simple practices, and its democratic flavor. Its chief adherents in the South in the early republic consisted largely of "frontier folk with a strong bias against the aristocracy."[24] "Many humble Christians" in the early republic, wrote Nathan Hatch, "yoked strenuous demands for revivals, in the name of George Whitefield, with calls for the expansion of popular sovereignty, in the name of the [American] Revolution." Relatively shorn of complex theological doctrine and elaborate liturgy and often delivered by revivalists with "coarse

language, earthy humor, biting sarcasm, and commonsense reasoning," evangelicalism appealed to the relatively uneducated but religiously sincere black and white folk of an overwhelmingly rural Georgia in the early nineteenth century and transformed the religious and cultural landscape of the state.[25] That push toward a more populist religious form, however, did not translate into a kind of Christian hyper-individualism. Even in Baptist congregations in Georgia, the community of believers—the church—"mediated the interpretation of scripture" so central to Evangelicals and thus grew as an important element of Christian life in rural Georgia; in a sense, the church had replaced the minister as the center of spiritual activity.[26] In doing so, it provided the impetus for the building of churches from one end of the state to the other in settings rural and urban.

Over time, evangelicalism grew more regularized and somewhat tamer, becoming entrenched in the fabric of the state, especially in the educational realm and in the mythology and practices surrounding the institution of

Penfield Baptist in Greene County, built in 1846, was the original home of Mercer University Chapel.

slavery. As a result of the rapid growth of adherents within the state, each of the main denominations founded educational institutions in the state in order to produce an educated ministry, and importantly all of them founded their institutions in rural Georgia. Presbyterians, who by the 1830s again began to gain adherents in the state, founded Oglethorpe University near the capital of Milledgeville, a relatively small town in the middle of a vast rural area. Methodists founded Emory College (now University) in Oxford, Georgia, thirty miles east of what was not yet the important urban center of Atlanta. Under the leadership of Adiel Sherwood and Jesse Mercer, Baptists founded Mercer Institute (now University) in the sleepy village of Penfield, halfway between Atlanta and Augusta and thirty miles south of Athens, the home of the University of Georgia. Importantly, Oglethorpe, Emory, and Mercer all later moved to the urban centers of Atlanta or Macon, but their founding in rural locations testifies to the essentially rural nature and dominance of evangelical Christianity in antebellum Georgia.

As Georgia transitioned from a frontier state to a cotton kingdom state in the middle decades of the nineteenth century, slavery, the institution that underpinned cotton agriculture, emerged as an issue to be debated, defended, and eventually fused with Christian expressions in Georgia. Many of the evangelicals who had come from the "powerless, defiant, lower class folk" had moved (or their children had) into a middle class more closely connected to the burgeoning market economy surrounding cotton, and as they did, they "became conservative defenders of much that they had criticized earlier, including slavery."[27] The egalitarianism of early southern evangelicalism "foundered on the intransigency of [slavery] in the South," and white Christians wrapped slavery in a biblical and evangelical protective covering.[28] In the same way that the abolitionist and antislavery movement in the North turned to biblical texts and Christian principles to argue against slavery, many southern Christians appealed to biblical texts that seemed to them to legitimize slavery and to other texts that encouraged slaves to obey their

After the war, when African Americans left Bark Camp Baptist to form their own church, membership dropped from 615 to 91.

masters, since by the middle of the nineteenth century, Scripture had become "the national book *par excellence*."[29] They also pointed to the many conversions of slaves that had taken place in the preceding decades and began to craft an argument that slavery actually benefitted these African descendants since it had been the mechanism by which they had been "exposed to the good news of Christianity and rescued from the 'heathenism' of Africa."[30]

Increasingly, the supporting ministers also argued that masters held an obligation to Christianize their slaves, though that Christianization seldom extended beyond conversion and preaching about submission. Charles Colcock Jones, for instance, turned his early discomfort with slavery into missionary work to slaves in Liberty County in the 1830s and proclaimed to local slave owners that "the great object for which we would communicate religious instruction to [the slaves] is that their souls may be saved. To this all other objects must be subordinated." Jones himself, though, provided those "other objects"— more passive and obedient slaves and more profit.[31] Indeed, the "motivation for bringing religious instruction to black slaves was . . . neither purely religious nor purely economic. On the contrary, religious and social forces were closely interwoven." Jones so convinced the local slave owners of both the righteousness and the efficacy of slave evangelization that they formed the "Liberty County Association for the Religious Instruction of the Negroes."[32] These masters, and many others, attempted to serve both God and Mammon through slave evangelization.

Black Christians turned to evangelical Christianity for succor in the midst of misery and for hope in the midst of darkness. Rejection of the master's religion might seem to make sense according to a modern reckoning, but many slaves instead chose to take the master's religion and adapt it to their purposes and needs, giving them agency in an important arena of their lives. Indeed, they largely "saw themselves carving out a religious sphere amid a cruel society that refused to recognize its own racial sins." Baptist and Methodist preachers in the early republic appealed to free and slave blacks because they "welcomed African-Americans as full participants in their communions and condemned the institution of slavery," they "proclaimed [a] Christianity that was fresh, capable of being readily understood and immediately experienced," and they welcomed "the emergence of black preachers and exhorters." When whites in the nineteenth century eventually restricted black participation in churches, black Christian slaves "retreated to their own private meetings in the slave quarters."[33] As Eugene Genovese observes, "Law or no, repression or no repression, the slaves heard their own black preachers, if not regularly, then at least frequently enough to make a difference in their lives." Despite the early efforts of white evangelicals to convert blacks, "the overwhelming number of black conversions grew from the efforts of African-American evangelists, not from the hands of white missionaries."[34]

These black evangelists combined useful elements of the American experiences such as democratization and religious freedom to help them "preserve elements of traditional African culture in their Christian practices."[35] In addition to certain theological orientations derived from their African heritage, blacks also incorporated "shouting and dancing" as well as the singing of spirituals that usually centered on biblical literature but allowed singers to "express their own very personal feelings about life and redemption."[36] Experience with Christianity also gave them experience within the church. Whether worshipping with whites, albeit in a separate section, or by themselves, they became familiar with the practices surrounding the life of a church—including the construction of church buildings. An uneasy tension between Christian brotherhood and white power increasingly limited slave or free black agency within white congregations, so a variety of arrangements emerged.[37] Jones, the Liberty County missionary to slaves, devised a plan whereby converted blacks would be part of the white church but also have the opportunity to worship on their own at "stations" (supervised by a white missionary) where they could "sing hymns and hear preaching adapted to their [as Jones put it] 'circumstances and conditions.'" At these stations, black Christian slaves might establish "a time and place for their own worship."[38] Some blacks did form separate churches, although mostly in urban areas among free blacks and mostly under the suspicious eye of white evangelicals.[39] By 1860, over 10 percent of the black population had joined a church, while many others worshipped the Christian God outside of church membership.[40] White and black evangelicals, then, used their Christianity to help them understand, explain, defend, and wrestle with the institution of slavery. For both whites and blacks, the Bible Belt both grew up alongside of and shaped the southern cotton kingdom of the early nineteenth century.

The Civil War ended the slave-based cotton kingdom but not the Bible Belt—in either the white or the black community. Despite crushing defeat by 1865—a defeat that might have soured white confidence in their Christian God—many white Christians constructed and then embraced a narrative of mythical proportions known as the Lost Cause, named after a book of that title published in Richmond in 1866 that exhorted southerners to maintain their separate identity even in the midst of defeat. The

St. Paul CME, in Hancock County, was originally organized on the Dickson Plantation in 1857.
This sanctuary was built on the same location in the 1870s.

basic story of the Lost Cause assured whites of the justice and righteousness of their efforts to defend slavery but condemned them for personal sins that led to the ultimate fall of the Confederacy. In much the same way that Old Testament prophets used defeat at the hands of pagan enemies to call the Hebrew people back to the worship of the true God, many Georgia ministers called whites back to worship in the church as a way to cleanse themselves from the sins that had caused their defeat.[41] They did not,

however, shoulder that other prophetic role from the Old Testament—the clarion call for social justice and for ethical action toward the poor and oppressed. As a result, the Lost Cause both "provided the model for segregation that the Southern churches accepted" and "failed to judge the society's racial patterns."[42] Blacks, freed from their oppressive masters, might have jettisoned Christianity as the religion of the slaveholding class but instead embraced the opportunity not only to participate in Christianity but also to assume leadership roles in their religion. Sadly, these two groups did not take the opportunity to work together to build unified denominations either among themselves or with their northern counterparts, instead using the postbellum period to reinforce or build separate denominational structures, North and South, white and black.

The two most numerous denominations in Georgia in the antebellum era—Baptists and Methodists—had split into separate southern and northern entities in the 1840s over some combination of theology and their approach to the issue of slavery. Georgians played leading roles in each of the schisms. In the case of the Methodists, debate over a Georgia bishop, James O. Andrew, holding slaves prompted the split. Northern Methodists objected and in 1844 pushed through a resolution instructing him to "desist from the exercise of his office so long as this impediment remains." Southern Methodists "took this as a signal that they must withdraw" and began making preparations for the creation of a Methodist Episcopal Church, South.[43] As for the Baptists, they split after the American Baptist Home Missionary Society refused in 1844 to sanction a slaveholding Georgian, James Reeves, as a missionary to an area of "religious destitution" in western Georgia. Less than a year later, the Southern Baptist Convention formed and held its first meeting in Augusta.[44]

After the war, the separate regional denominations continued apart despite abortive efforts to reunite the two wings of the denominations. Hard feelings, theological differences, and different approaches to the newly freed slaves hindered any rapprochement. Blacks found themselves forced to choose either between trying to integrate into the southern churches, which normally treated them as paternalistically as they had in the antebellum era, connect with the fairly minimal efforts of the northern churches to reengage in the south, or form their own churches and denominations. A pattern of "negotiation, contestation, and confrontation" between black and white evangelicals took place in the era of

Reconstruction that reshaped southern denominationalism.[45] Never fully at home in the numerous southern white churches or the few northern churches, black Methodists and later black Baptists formed their own denominations. Black Methodists split first, forming two groups in the first decade after the end of the war, the African Methodist Episcopal (AME) Church and the Colored Methodist Episcopal (CME) Church. The first formed more as a grassroots entity out of the black Methodist community and found leadership in Georgia from Henry McNeal Turner, a freeborn South Carolinian Methodist minister who had spent much of the war in Washington, D.C. After the war he organized a "missionary campaign" to help freedmen take charge of their own lives, education, and religion.[46] Turner "emphasized the blackness of the AME and taunted free people who attended white churches."[47] The CME formed with the assistance of the southern Methodist church and under the leadership in Georgia of Lucius Holsey, "the most remarkable of the church's early leaders." These two denominations experienced a "strained" relationship for much of the postbellum era, with the AME being frustrated by the CME's apolitical stance, its "cordial relationship with white Methodists[,] and its readiness to accommodate white supremacy."[48] Nevertheless, both churches established an important presence in rural and urban Georgia, and both churches had a strong monistic orientation that blurred the modern lines between secular and sacred and that produced a dynamic whereby churches served "both religious and social ends, with the black minister playing not only a strong spiritual but also community role."[49] The Baptists did not finally split until the 1890s, partly because the congregational nature of Baptist church governance allowed for black congregations to exercise a higher degree of independence. Eventually though, chafing under the racism of the Georgia and Southern Baptist conventions, black Georgia Baptists helped form the National Baptist Convention in Atlanta in 1895.[50] Extraordinarily, "right in the midst of these upheavals and maneuverings, throngs of African Americans converted" to evangelical Christianity in an event that one historian has dubbed "the African-American Great Awakening." These conversions caused the numbers of black churchgoers to mushroom and "cemented evangelicalism as the central component of African-American religious life."[51] Thus white and black Georgia Christians retained and even expanded their religious footprint in the Postbellum era, but sadly by and large voluntarily worshipped in as segregated a manner as the coming Jim Crow South legally segregated the rest of southern life.

No matter the denomination, no matter the era, Georgia Christians built churches. The exact nature of the buildings varied somewhat from era to era, denomination to denomination, and rural to urban. From Georgia's official Anglican founding, through its pluralistic colonial period, and into its evangelical phase, Georgia Christians used wood, stone, and glass to erect houses of worship suited to their needs and theological inclinations. Rural churches, reflecting local supplies and somewhat more meager resources compared to their urban brethren, tended to be constructed mostly of wood rather than brick or stone, and as a result many have not survived into the twenty-first century. Since evangelicals of one sort or another founded most of the churches, their style tended to be fairly plain—rectangular (not cruciform) in shape with flat-topped windows, some with a steeple or tower pointing to heaven, some not, and many with a triangular pediment or columns or both—referencing the trinity in the case of the former and in both cases the then-popular Greek Revival style that "permeated all levels of building, from folk-style to the high style, architect-designed buildings."[52] Many churches that have survived no longer have functioning congregations, much of rural Georgia having migrated to urban areas in the late twentieth century. Nevertheless, the buildings that remain testify to the commitment, variety, and endurance of Georgia Christians, white and black, rich and poor, sophisticated and simple. Georgia's churches also reflected and reflect the rich, complex, and often painful history of the state in its first century and a half.

NOTES

The epigraph is from Jeanne Halgren Kilde, *When Church Became Theatre: The Transformation of Evangelical Architecture and Worship in Nineteenth-Century America* (Oxford: Oxford University Press, 2002), 10.

1. Bishop David Arias, *Spanish Cross in Georgia* (Lanham, Md.: University Press of America, 1994) effectively describes Spanish missionary and church-building efforts in sixteenth- and seventeenth-century "Georgia."

2. "Charter of the Colony," in *The Colonial Records of the State of Georgia*, ed. Allen D. Candler, 26 vols. (Atlanta: Franklin Printing and Publishing Co., 1904), 1:11–26, quotation on 21.

3. Reba Carolyn Strickland, *Religion and State in Georgia in the Eighteenth Century* (New York: Columbia University Press, 1939), 27–36.

4. Harvey H. Jackson, "Parson and Squire: James Oglethorpe and the Role of the Anglican Church in Georgia, 1733–1736," in *Oglethorpe in Perspective: Georgia's Founder after Two Hundred Years*, eds. Phinizy Spalding and Harvey H. Jackson (Tuscaloosa: University of Alabama Press, 1989), 44–65, provides a useful overview of the experiences of the early Anglican ministers to Georgia, especially in regards to their relationship with Oglethorpe.

5. Julie Anne Sweet provides a good, basic retelling of Anglican priestly troubles in the years between the Wesleys' departure and Zouberbuhler's arrival in *William Stephens: Georgia's Forgotten Founder* (Baton Rouge: Louisiana State University Press, 2010), 178–200. The first three chapters of Edward J. Cashin, *Beloved Bethesda: A History of George Whitefield's Home for Boys, 1740–2000* (Macon, Ga.: Mercer University Press, 2001), provide a sound retelling of the early years of the Bethesda Orphanage.

6. Wayne Mixon, "Georgia," in *Religion in the Southern States: A Historical Study*, ed. Samuel S. Hill (Macon, Ga.: Mercer University Press, 1983), 77–100, quotation on 78. Strickland, *Religion and State in Georgia in the Eighteenth Century*, 100–138, examines the main ecclesiastical currents of the royal period.

7. George Fenwick Jones, *The Georgia Dutch: From the Rhine and Danube to the Savannah, 1733–1783* (Athens: University of Georgia Press, 1992), provides the best overview of the Lutheran experience.

8. Adelaide Fries, *Moravians in Georgia, 1735–1740* (Raleigh, N.C.: Edwards and Broughton, 1905), still provides the most thorough treatment of the Moravian experience in Georgia.

9. Anthony W. Parker, *Scottish Highlanders in Colonial Georgia: The Recruitment, Emigration, and Settlement at Darien, 1735–1748* (Athens: University of Georgia Press, 1997) details the history of the colonial Darien settlement.

10. Mixon, "Georgia," 79–81, and David S. Williams, *From Mounds to Megachurches: Georgia's Religious Heritage* (Athens: University of Georgia Press, 2008), 19–24, provide basic information about the multiplicity of religious groups that settled in colonial Georgia.

11. Gloria Sampson, *Historic Churches and Temples of Georgia* (Macon, Ga.: Mercer University Press, 1987), 14.

12. D. Williams, *Mounds to Megachurches*, 23.

13. Ibid., 32.

14. See Strickland, *Religion and State in Georgia in the Eighteenth Century*, 139–160, for a rundown of the positions of leading ministers and groups in Georgia in relation to the American Revolution. She estimates that the statewide fighting and division prompted by the Revolution had left "organized religion . . . practically non-existent in Georgia in 1782." (160). Mixon concurs, stating bluntly that "the American Revolution stopped the progress of organized religion in Georgia." Mixon, "Georgia," 81.

15. Eric Schlereth, *An Age of Infidels: The Politics of Religious Controversy in the Early United States* (Philadelphia: University of Pennsylvania Press, 2013), 36–37 and 116.

16. Martin E. Marty, a leading scholar of U.S. religion, has even argued that "there has been a symbiosis between unfolding modernity and developing Evangelicalism." See Martin E. Marty, "The Revival of Evangelicalism and Southern Religion," in *Varieties of Southern Evangelicalism*, ed. David Edwin Harrell Jr. (Macon, Ga.: Mercer University Press, 1981), 7–21, quotation on 9.

17. Marty, "Revival of Evangelicalism and Southern Religion," 10.

18. John B. Boles, *The Great Revival, 1787–1805* (Lexington: University of Kentucky Press, 1972), 183.

19. Bruce R. Dickson Jr., *And They All Sang Hallelujah: Plain-Folk Camp-Meeting Religion, 1800–1845* (Knoxville: University of Tennessee Press, 1974), 61.

20. Christine Heyrman, *Southern Cross: The Beginnings of the Bible Belt* (Chapel Hill: University of North Carolina Press, 1997), 4.

21. Dickson, *And They All Sang Hallelujah*, 61–95, provides a good description of the activities and experiences at a camp meeting.

22. Mixon, "Georgia," 82, 88.

23. Heyrman, *Southern Cross*, 19.

24. Wayne Flynt, "One in the Spirit, Many in the Flesh: Southern Evangelicals," in Harrell, *Varieties of Southern Evangelicalism*, 23–44, quotation on 24.

25. Nathan O. Hatch, *The Democratization of American Christianity* (New Haven: Yale University Press, 1989), 6–7, 34.

26. Gregory A. Wills, *Democratic Religion: Freedom, Authority, and Church Discipline in the Baptist South, 1785–1900* (New York: Oxford University Press, 1997), provides a detailed description of how "Southern

Baptists established a spirituality that was at once democratic and authoritarian." This "democratic religion" he argues, was "as much medieval as it was modern." Quotations here and in text on viii.

27. Flynt, "One in the Spirit, Many in the Flesh," 24–25.

28. Albert J. Raboteau, *Slave Religion: The "Invisible Institution" in the Antebellum South* (New York: Oxford University Press, 1978), 145.

29. Mark Noll, in "The Bible and Slavery," in *Religion and the American Civil War*, eds. Randall M. Miller, Harry S. Stout, and Charles Wilson Reagan (Oxford: Oxford University Press, 1998), 43–73, provides a detailed overview of how both sides interpreted Biblical texts to support or condemn slavery; quotation on 48.

30. D. Williams, *Mounds to Megachurches*, 56–59, quotation on 56.

31. Charles Colcock Jones quoted in Erskine Clark, *Wrestlin' Jacob: A Portrait of Religion in the Old South* (Atlanta: John Knox Press, 1979), 27.

32. Clark, *Wrestlin' Jacob*, 105, 28.

33. Hatch, *Democratization of American Christianity*, 102–105, 112.

34. Eugene D. Genovese, *Roll, Jordan, Roll: The World the Slaves Made* (New York: Vintage, 1976), 257.

35. Jay Riley Case, *An Unpredictable Gospel: American Evangelicals and World Christianity, 1812–1920* (Oxford: Oxford University Press, 2012), 159–160.

36. William E. Montgomery, *Under Their Own Vine and Fig Tree: The African-American Church in the South, 1865–1900* (Baton Rouge: Louisiana State University Press, 1993), 15–16.

37. Raboteau, *Slave Religion*, 179–180.

38. Clark, *Wrestlin' Jacob*, 29–30.

39. Montgomery, *Under Their Own Vine and Fig Tree*, 28.

40. Mixon, "Georgia," 86.

41. D. Williams, *Mounds to Megachurches*, 72–76, provides an overview of how the Lost Cause played out in churches in Georgia.

42. Charles Reagan Wilson, *Baptized in Blood: The Religion of the Lost Cause, 1865–1920* (Athens: University of Georgia Press, 1980), 16. *The Myth of the Lost Cause and Civil War History*, eds. Gary W. Gallagher and Alan T. Nolan (Bloomington: Indiana University Press, 2000), examines the Lost Cause and its effects on southern culture from a variety of angles.

43. Quotation from the *Journal of the General Conference* (1844) taken from C. C. Goen, *Broken Churches, Broken Nation: Denominational Schisms and the Coming of the American Civil War* (Macon, Ga.: Mercer University Press, 1985), 83. The subsequent quotation is from Goen, *Broken Churches, Broken Nation*, 83.

44. Robert G. Gardner, *A Decade of Debate and Division: Georgia Baptists and the Formation of the Southern Baptist Convention* (Macon, Ga.: Mercer University Press, 1995), 13–19, quotation on 13.

45. Case, *Unpredictable Gospel*, 162.

46. Montgomery, *Under Their Own Vine and Fig Tree*, 50–51, 60, quotation on 60.

47. Donald L. Grant, *The Way It Was in the South: The Black Experience in Georgia* (New York: Birch Lane Press, 1993), 268.

48. Montgomery, *Under Their Own Vine and Fig Tree*, 122, 123.

49. D. Williams, *Mounds to Megachurches*, 82.

50. Mixon, "Georgia," 89–90, and D. Williams, *Mounds to Megachurches*, 76–83, provide brief overviews of the postbellum ecclesiastical divisions within the Baptist and Methodist churches in Georgia.

51. Case, *Unpredictable Gospel*, 162–163.

52. Quotation from Jeffery Howe, *Houses of Worship: An Identification Guide to the History and Styles of American Religious Architecture* (San Diego: Thunder Bay Press, 2003), 154; the rectangular shape represented an older form of church building than the medieval cruciform shape so closely identified in Evangelicals' minds with Roman Catholicism and established churches; see Howe, introduction, *Houses of Worship*. See Louis P. Nelson, *The Beauty of Holiness: Anglicanism and Architecture in Colonial South Carolina* (Chapel Hill: University of North Carolina Press, 2008), 147–148, for a brief discussion of dissenter versus establishment approaches toward church building, and Peter W. Williams, *Houses of God: Region, Religion, and Architecture in the United States* (Urbana: University of Illinois Press, 1997), 119–121, for a brief discussion of southern Evangelical appropriation of the Greek Revival style, so universal that Peter Williams described it as "vernacular" for the "widely scattered rural frame churches" of the South (120).

Banks County	*Hebron Presbyterian*
Banks County	*Mt. Olivet Methodist*
Ben Hill County	*Young's Chapel Methodist*
Brantley County	*High Bluff Primitive Baptist*
Brooks County	*Liberty Baptist*
Brooks County	*Bethlehem Primitive Baptist*
Burke County	*Bark Camp Baptist*
Camden County	*First Presbyterian of St. Marys*
Chattooga County	*Alpine Presbyterian*
Cherokee County	*Fields Chapel United Methodist*
Columbia County	*Kiokee Baptist*
Effingham County	*Jerusalem Lutheran*
Floyd County	*Sardis Presbyterian*
Franklin County	*Carroll's Methodist*
Greene County	*Bethesda Baptist*
Greene County	*Penfield Baptist*
Habersham County	*Grace-Calvary Episcopal*
Hancock County	*Powelton Baptist*
Hancock County	*Powelton Methodist*
Hancock County	*St. Paul CME*
Jackson County	*Apple Valley Baptist*
Jackson County	*Thyatira Presbyterian*
Jasper County	*Concord Primitive Baptist*
Jenkins County	*Big Buckhead Baptist*
Jenkins County	*Carswell Grove Baptist*
Jones County	*Clinton Methodist*
Liberty County	*Midway Congregational*
McDuffie County	*Wrightsboro Methodist*
McIntosh County	*Sapelo First African Baptist*
McIntosh County	*St. Cyprian's Episcopal*
Mitchell County	*Mt. Enon Baptist*
Oglethorpe County	*Beth Salem Presbyterian*
Oglethorpe County	*Philomath Presbyterian*
Polk County	*Van Wert Methodist*
Randolph County	*Benevolence Baptist*
Stewart County	*Antioch Primitive Baptist*
Sumter County	*Plains Baptist*
Sumter County	*St. Mark's Lutheran*
Taliaferro County	*Antioch Baptist*
Taliaferro County	*Locust Grove Catholic*
Walker County	*Cove Methodist*
Ware County	*Ezekiel New Congregational Methodist*
Ware County	*Old Ruskin*
Warren County	*Barnett Methodist*
Warren County	*Fountain Campground*
White County	*Crescent Hill Baptist*
Wilkes County	*Friendship Baptist*

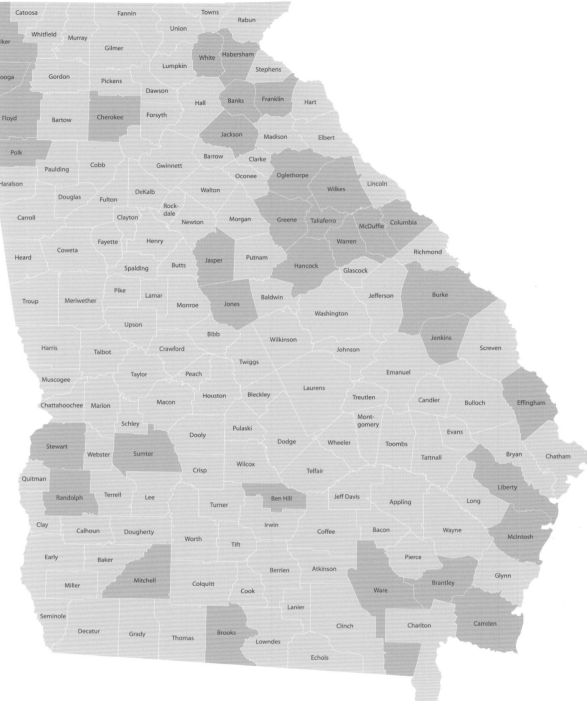

Historic Rural Churches of Georgia

Hebron Presbyterian

Consisting of a meetinghouse, schoolhouse, and cemetery, this Presbyterian church on the northwestern frontier of Georgia is a result of postrevolutionary Scots-Irish immigration. When the original church structure, a log cabin, was built in 1797, the Cherokees had recently ceded the land that became Banks County in the Long Swamp Treaty of 1783.

The little church prospered, necessitating a new church building for the growing congregation in 1800, and in 1805 the owner of the property deeded 7 acres over to the church in return for a payment of ten cents. A simple frame structure with shutters over the window openings was erected where the old one stood. Continued growth of the church resulted in the third and current structure, built in 1884.

As was typical in the Georgia backcountry where there were no courthouses and few lawyers, churches performed many community roles, among them conflict resolution and policing the behavior of the congregants. Some transgressions were serious, whereas others seem trivial by modern standards. For example, in 1893 members were suspended from the church for the serious offense of holding a Christmas party and dancing there— such punishment was not to be taken lightly in the backcountry. Only true repentance before their peers would gain the offenders readmittance to the community.

The middle decades of the twentieth century saw the introduction of electricity (1940s), gas heat (1951), and restrooms (1969). A brief history by Charles Toney, *Hebron Presbyterian Church: God's Pilgrim People 1796–1996*, is a helpful pamphlet on the church, on the sturdy Scottish Highlanders who settled around Hebron, and on those who came after them. Hebron Presbyterian continues an active ministry.

This third church home for Hebron Presbyterian has been standing since 1884. Although the interior has been outfitted with modern conveniences, the wide wallboards and ceiling boards are original.

This Communion table is one of two original to the first church.
More than two hundred years ago, craftsmen cut a single plank
with a pit saw, leaving long irregular saw marks that run parallel
to the grain. Rather than pound in nails, craftsmen fashioned
dovetail, mortise-and-tenon joints. Displaying and using relics like
these helps the congregation and visitors appreciate and respect
the church's history.

In most rural Georgia churches prior to 1865, slaves sat in
separate galleries or in the back of the church on benches.
Originally, this simple bench constructed from wide pine
boards seated slaves worshipping at the same service as
their owners.

On the early Georgia frontier, the upright fieldstone grave markers were often
all families could afford. However, the substantial grave house of stone over
the final resting place of this unnamed child indicates a family of some wealth.

Stone grave houses of this type were common in Scotland and Ireland. In the
foreground are grave markers for Revolutionary War soldiers who moved here
in order to take advantage of the postwar settlement offer. Due to the nature
of the land, farming was much harder in the northern part of the state and
required tough pioneers willing to do it.

A schoolhouse at Hebron was established in the 1830s. Occupying a crude log structure twenty feet square, the school was well attended and served both the white and black communities. Slaves were taught to read with the permission of their masters in the school's early days, but that ceased in the 1850s with the Georgia General Assembly's passage of a law prohibiting the education of slaves. A larger single-story structure was built in 1855 and then replaced with this two-story building in 1890.

Mt. Olivet Methodist

Mt. Olivet Methodist's history goes back to the Reverend Francis Marion Ragsdale and the Ragsdale Mill. Born in 1822, Marion Ragsdale was named after one of his father's heroes, Francis Marion, the Swamp Fox of Revolutionary War fame. Ragsdale was an entrepreneur and was listed in the 1850 census as a mechanic. The first mill was built on Nail's Creek sometime before 1837. Ragsdale acquired the mill site and 257 acres of land from his father in 1853 and established the present Ragsdale Mill, which today stands on church property.

In the Civil War era, a rift occurred within the Methodist Church over the issue of slavery. The Ragsdales did not approve of slavery and split from Mt. Pleasant Methodist over the issue, resulting in the founding of Mt. Olivet. In 1868, Ragsdale's neighbor, William Hix, deeded to the trustees of Mt. Olivet a 5½-acre church lot, upon which the good reverend built the church, performing many marriages and baptisms there in the 1870s and 1880s.

A visionary, Ragsdale intended to establish a town to be called Nail's Creek. The first step of his plan was to build a Grange hall on the property in 1883 that also served as a schoolhouse. The Grange is a farmers' organization that furthers agricultural knowledge and best practices within the community. Ragsdale envisioned all of these structures to lie at the center of the town of Nail's Creek. Alas, time passed and the development never came to fruition.

The last regular church service at Mt. Olivet was in 1961. It is now used for weddings, occasional religious purposes, and the annual Old Fashioned Day in May. The church has been carefully maintained by its present owners.

Mt. Olivet is an extraordinary example of rural skill and craftsmanship, and Francis Marion Ragsdale was a master craftsman. The raised, semicircular chancel with its delicate, turned balustrade is a marked contrast to the sturdy pews constructed just after the Civil War from pine timber harvested, hand-planed, and joined nearby.

Ragsdale avoided interior visible supports such as walls and columns by employing a structural technique known as the trussed-rafter roof design— two equal inclined planes joined by a central, level panel. The ceiling is supported by suspension trusses, using the same principle as a suspension bridge. The large twelve-over-twelve windows made possible by the high ceilings pour light into this space.

Produced by the Cornish Company of Washington, New Jersey,
established in 1879, this decorative foot-pedal organ would have
represented a significant expense when it was new.

The Reverend Francis Marion Ragsdale died in 1888. The final resting place of the founder of Ragsdale Mill, Mt. Olivet Church, and the township of Nail's Creek is marked by a marble monument made in a style popular in the late nineteenth and early twentieth centuries. The arch linking the two pillars signifies the union of Francis Marion and Martha Ragsdale in marriage, death, and heaven.

Ragsdale Mill used the water's 30-foot drop over a granite ledge to generate power. According to local lore, when asked why he was going to the trouble of building the mill with dovetail joints for extra strength, the reverend replied, "After I'm gone, I want people to know that somebody has been here."

Young's Chapel Methodist

BEN HILL COUNTY   ORG. CA. 1875

Located on a dirt road in a largely agricultural part of south-central Georgia, this church was part of the local community for a century before its congregation dwindled in the mid-1970s. Abandonment of the church eventually created the forlorn relic visible here. Efforts early in the second decade of the twenty-first century to rekindle interest and raise funds for restoration have, as yet, been unsuccessful.

The history of Young's Chapel Methodist Church begins around 1875 as a brush arbor church in what was then known as Ashley. Having established itself here, the congregation built this structure of lumber made from locally harvested heart pine. When member John Thomas Young donated land for the chapel and a cemetery near what is now the town of Rebecca, the building was moved the few miles to its current location.

The chapel still bears the name of benefactor John Thomas Young, whose family continuously worshiped and served here while also contributing to the community and the state, providing civic service through several generations.

Behind the chapel is a small, rather informal burial ground. The earliest known burials date from 1908, and burials continued into the twenty-first century. Of the thirty-eight interments, eighteen are from the Young family.

We are indebted to Sherri Butler's informative piece in the *Fitzgerald Herald-Ledger* for background on this church.

Time and the elements have taken their toll on this chapel since its closure in the mid-1970s. The quiet simplicity of this old building, as evidenced in the primitive, wooden bench pews and the locally sourced materials, speaks eloquently of an agrarian lifestyle and the hard work that goes with it.

With a sound roof and tight windows, heart-pine structures, even unpainted, can last a very long time. The double threat of a leaking roof and broken window panes along Young's Chapel's south wall have accelerated deterioration inside and out. Young's Chapel is in dire need of attention.

The simplest chancel, encircled by leather-bound kneelers, served the congregation for a century. What might have been an apse appears to be boarded over. One of John Thomas Young's descendants, Emma Young, tells us she provided accompaniment on this piano for many years.

PHOTOGRAPHY BY RANDALL DAVIS

High Bluff Primitive Baptist

High Bluff exemplifies the architecture of the historic Wiregrass Primitive Baptist churches, most of which are located in a small region of Southeast and Southwest Georgia, with a few in North Florida. High Bluff was organized in 1819 by Isham Peacock, a legend among the Wiregrass Primitives. Having served in the American Revolution, Elder Peacock began his religious life in 1802 at the remarkable old age of sixty, retiring from Providence Church in Ware County in 1844 at 101. In the interim he pastored and helped establish Primitive Baptist churches in South Georgia and North Florida. Typical of the Primitive Baptist preachers of the early nineteenth century, he was not a man of letters, but he was adept at preaching to and converting the wild frontier cattle drovers who populated this part of Georgia.

Nine members constituted High Bluff Primitive Baptist Church in September 1819 in a settlement on a high bluff (hence the name) of the south bank of the Satilla River. Ministers Isham Peacock and Fleming Bates constituted the presbytery of the church. The congregation built a meetinghouse, established a burial ground, and chose Bates as their pastor in 1821.

A group of members elected to constitute a church at Kettle Creek in 1823, and a few years later the remaining members voted to join the church at Big Creek, some twenty miles away. We are told there was a cholera outbreak within the community at that time. This was in an era before the causes of cholera were understood, and out of fear, the congregation chose to abandon High Bluff Church. In fact, the entire High Bluff area was vacated. Sometime in the late 1870s, Big Creek Church was renamed High Bluff, thereby honoring the original church.

High Bluff still meets and welcomes a small congregation, currently every second weekend of the month.

For more information regarding this subdenomination within the Primitive Baptist tradition, see Bethlehem Primitive Baptist Church (page 39). Also refer to John Crowley's *Primitive Baptists of the Wiregrass South: 1815 to Present.*

Wiregrass Primitive Baptist churches are similar in appearance because they all follow, and adhere rigidly, to a strict doctrine of no frills and no ornamentation. Within this tradition, the sanctuary must not distract the congregation from the principal task of worship, as evidenced here.

The starkness of the unfinished wood throughout the interior is even more evident in this black-and-white photograph, which also accentuates and reveals the open-attic frame construction found in each of the Wiregrass Primitive buildings. Note the eye-pleasing, skeletal geometry of the wooden ceiling beams and the cross bracing.

This utilitarian pulpit is characteristic of the Wiregrass Primitive Baptist style and demonstrates the congregation's adherence to traditions that began in the early 1800s.

Of more than two thousand interments in the High Bluff cemetery, at least 250 are of the Griffin family. These gravestones stand above the remains of John and Peter Griffin, who served with the Twenty-Sixth Georgia Infantry during the Civil War. According to their service records, John was wounded on August 28, 1862, at Second Manassas and died on September 5. Ironically, his brother, Peter, had been discharged on "disability" at Richmond on August 16, 1862—not even two weeks before his brother was mortally wounded.

Big Creek had already been renamed High Bluff when the Ammons brothers died in 1888. Brainard Ammons, who died at the age of three and a half on November 14, 1888, lies beside his brother, Owen, who preceded him in death by twelve days. Infant deaths were very common in the backcountry, but, coming so close together, we think these toddlers' deaths might have resulted from an epidemic.

Liberty Baptist

To reach Liberty Baptist Church, one travels along a rural road that is a mixture of red dirt and white sand, flanked by large oaks festooned with Spanish moss. Round a slight curve in the old road and suddenly this stunning and majestic rural church comes into view.

The history of Liberty Baptist begins in a time of conflict within the South Georgia Baptist community. Sometime in the 1830s, the Primitive Baptists in this part of the state struggled to come to grips with new ministries emerging in some of its churches. In 1841, the denomination's governing body passed a highly restrictive (some might say reactionary) article that essentially excommunicated any member practicing, or even believing, in any of the new activities (see more about the Wiregrass Primitive tradition at the Bethlehem entry, page 39).

Nancy Hagan, a member of Mount Moriah Church, which ascribed to the new restrictions, took issue with this article, which prohibited, among other things, Sunday school instruction and missionary work. Hagan formally withdrew from her church, joining a handful of others in the community who shared her views. The tiny congregation named their church Liberty and evidently initially worshipped in a vacant church nearby.

The current structure is the second home of Liberty Baptist. In 1857, the trustees of Liberty moved that a new church be built in nearby Grooverville. The resulting 40-by-50-foot Greek Revival building features an entrance portico supported by heart-pine columns and topped by a bell tower. Liberty, both architecturally and theologically, was a dramatic departure from Wiregrass Primitives.

Metal cuspidors were positioned about the sanctuary as, "some of the brethren used tobacco freely," according to the church's centennial pamphlet. From 1844 until just after the Civil War, black members worshipped from stepped pews in the deep gallery. The first service held in this splendid new building was in June 1858, and over the years a number of members fulfilled the founders' missionary vocation.

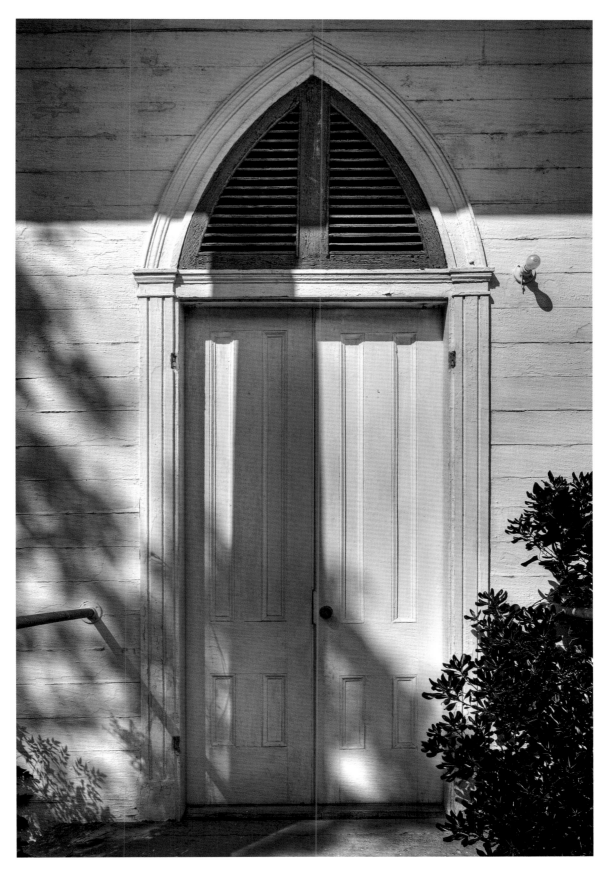

The front entrance to Liberty Baptist has not changed materially since 1858. The styling, millwork, fit, finish, and well-formed Gothic arch enclosing the heart-pine, four-panel doors are impeccable.

The pair of columns supporting the gallery draws the eye toward the elegant white pulpit. Simple pews and the Gothic arches collaborate to create a peaceful and reverential mood.

Slave galleries such as the one visible here were common in prosperous white churches built before the Civil War. According to church history, black slaves were accepted as members from 1844 until after the Civil War, when they formed their own churches. That the slave gallery extends over more than half of the lower-level pews hints at the high number of slaves in proportion to white members when this church was finished in 1858.

As seen from the slave gallery, the altar area and these
windows reiterate the sophistication of the mid-1800s design
and decorative elements at Liberty. The Gothic wood panels
flanking the modest chancel mimic the window and door styles
that recur throughout the church. Note that the lower halves of
the windows have interior as well as exterior shutters.

Craftsmanship, fine materials, and a blend of both Gothic and Greek revival architecture converge in Liberty Baptist Church to create a South Georgia architectural masterpiece that has been well cared for by the Grooverville community for over 150 years.

Bethlehem Primitive Baptist

BROOKS COUNTY   ORG. 1834

What you see here is a magnificent example of a Wiregrass Primitive Baptist Church, named after the native grass *Aristida stricta* (wiregrass) so prevalent in the South Georgia ecosystem. Wiregrass Primitive Baptist churches were prolific in South Georgia in the early 1800s, and some remain active churches today. The basic design always involved a building low to the ground with unpainted wood, a single-gable roof without a steeple and basic window and door framing—in essence, completely functional and austere.

The Primitive Baptists were suspicious of anything new and nontraditional, especially if espoused by those they perceived to be of a higher social class. In 1841, a major split occurred within the southern Baptist churches because of differences of opinion regarding religious doctrine and stewardship, as John Crowley describes in *Primitive Baptists of the Wiregrass South: 1815 to Present*: "In 1841 the Ocklochnee anti-Missionary Baptist Association added an article to their original Articles of Faith making the famous Thirteenth Article, in which they declared non-fellowship with any member who engaged or believed in Sunday-school work, missions, theological schools or any other new-fangled institutions of the day." Nothing personifies this conflict more than this church and the beautiful church in nearby Grooverville, Liberty Baptist (see page 29), only a few miles away.

The first church the Bethlehem congregation built after organizing in November 1834 was a log meetinghouse about a mile from here on the property of John Dukes. The slave gallery there was purported to be the only one in any of the South Georgia Primitive Baptist churches. That is not surprising because the Georgia Wiregrass ecosystem is not conducive to cotton cultivation, so there were very few slaves in this region.

Although elsewhere in the South few churches were built during the war, this relatively isolated church resolved in February 1861 to look for a new location, finding one about a mile away. Shortly after, they dismantled the church and used the materials to build the present church on the new site.

Both the church and cemetery were added to the National Register of Historic Places in 2004. Although the church seems to have been out of use for some time, the cemetery remained in use into the twenty-first century.

The style of the main entrance to the sanctuary articulates the
builders' commitment to Wiregrass Primitive doctrine, which
eschewed ostentatious and newfangled accoutrements.

Most Wiregrass Primitive churches were built of posts
and beams held together with an elaborate system of pegs.
Until the ceiling was added in 1940, the view from the
pulpit took in exposed rafters.

The mass and scale of the pulpit in contrast to the low pews make a powerful visual statement to accompany a stern sermon. The low bench in front of the pulpit seated the clerk and moderator, who were present for every service.

Positioning the pews close to the unadorned, simply
framed twelve-over-twelve windows provides ample
sunlight by which to read the Bible. Using heart-pine
boards 10 to 12 inches wide was an effective way to reduce
the time and labor needed to saw and lay the floor.

The time-honored post-and-beam construction technique is simple and requires the least fastening hardware (in this case, just two wooden pegs). Unadorned, cheap, simple, and very effective: these pillars remain plumb and square.

The old outhouse, or comfort station, at Bethlehem preserved the spartan theme of the Wiregrass Primitive Baptists well into the twentieth century.

Bark Camp Baptist

Bark Camp Baptist is one of the oldest churches in the Georgia backcountry, having been established in 1788 by twenty-nine people, including its first pastor, Miles Scarboro. Historian John K. Derden identifies Bark Camp Baptist as having been a "Plantation district church," noting that in the postrevolutionary period "available land and fertile soil attracted settlers to the area and eventually led to the creation of a number of prosperous plantations in the area."

The congregation's first two structures were log, and the third was frame. However, the affinity of early wealthy planters in Burke County for well-built, Greek revival sanctuaries is evident in the current structure, built in 1848. At that time, the majority of Bark Camp congregants were black slaves. After the Civil War, black members worked with the Bark Camp Baptist leadership to form their own church. When they left in 1867, membership here plummeted from 615 to 91.

Bark Camp closed its doors in 1958 as the community dwindled and the younger generation moved away. In 1959 it was listed by the Hephzibah Baptist Association as defunct. Its legacy includes having contributed to the formation of a handful of churches, including the new Bark Camp Baptist Church established by black members, which remains active. As Derden says, this church "lives on through its spiritual offspring."

The family of Leonard Quick belonged to the church in the 1940s and 1950s, and in 1953 Leonard was ordained at Bark Camp. After his retirement, Quick returned to Bark Camp and founded a nonprofit group that set about restoring the church. The resulting Bark Camp Church Association maintains the property, which is now open for special events and services.

Parishioners entering the church through the main entrance, with its columned portico, find themselves in the front of the sanctuary, with choir seats on either side of the doors. A raised chancel presides over a simple but sturdy sanctuary. The tall walls and ceilings are made of the usual wide, horizontal pine boards; moldings are quite plain.

The floor, the pews, and the horizontal wallboards were hand hewn from local Georgia longleaf pine. The pew backs consist of two wide boards, while the seats are formed from only one board. The pine trees predominant in this area in 1857 were hundreds of years old, far older and larger than most early settlers had seen elsewhere in the colonies. Such old-growth forests are now long gone from the region.

Wide-planked floors, simple pews and high ceilings project the strength and simple elegance of the sanctuary. Although not original, the kerosene lamps atop wooden wall brackets evoke more atmosphere than the electric pendant lighting.

The Burtons were among the most prominent early pioneer families in Burke County, and their gravestones reflect the wealth that had been created by the family. Susan Burton was the matriarch. Three of the family headstones belong to her sons who served in the Civil War. Only one son survived the war. James was killed in action on July 2 at Gettysburg, and Charles, according to Findagrave, "died from exhaustion in retreat from Atlanta near McDonough, GA." He was seventeen.

Within this wrought-iron fence lie the remains of a prominent and prosperous early
Georgia family, the Inmans. Jeriamiah Shadrach Inman's father was Alfred, and his
grandfather and great-grandfather were Daniel and Shadrach Inman. The Inmans had
migrated from North Carolina into Tennessee and then into Georgia.

PHOTOGRAPHY BY WAYNE MOORE

First Presbyterian of St. Marys

CAMDEN COUNTY   ORG. 1808

One of the oldest Presbyterian meetinghouses in the state of Georgia, the First Presbyterian Church of St. Marys is a stunning example of tidewater architecture. In 1807 and 1808, monies were raised locally to build a nondenominational church for the residents of the town, and this structure was built in 1808. According to church history, a Presbyterian missionary arrived at the church in 1821 and, finding the local practice of religion to be in a "very low and languishing state, having existence in name only," he set about mending the problem. The congregation apparently took to the young man, ordaining him as their first pastor in 1822 and formally committing to the Presbyterian denomination.

The church is a perfect complement to the historic village of St. Marys, which is separated from Florida by the St. Marys River. A Timucuan Native American village originally lay here but was probably abandoned before Georgia became a British colony. The earliest residents of the modern town were probably Acadians, who arrived via Hispaniola in 1791. After the American Revolution, this area was part of the estate confiscated from two Royalists, brothers of the British governor James Wright.

Rather than springing up on its own, the eventual town of St. Marys was the result of a visionary state legislator, Jacob Weed, who came to own the land. Weed gathered nineteen other men into a plan in 1788 to establish the town on a 1,672-acre patch along the meandering river. Owned by the twenty, this early planned town was dotted with public squares. According to the *New Georgia Encyclopedia*, "each one of the twenty founders was authorized to use the squares and received a mixture of good, marshy land in his purchase."

The church, now part of the Savannah Presbytery, has several hundred members and an active ministry. Although the general area has grown in recent years, the old village of St. Marys remains much the same as in years past.

One enters the sanctuary by ascending the western staircase to the open
vestibule at the base of the center steeple. Most early churches built for
Methodist or Baptist congregations had two front doors, one for men and the
other for women and children. However, since this was chartered and built in
1808 as a nondenominational place of worship for the citizens of St. Marys,
the meetinghouse has only one wide entrance door.

This small meetinghouse invokes a sense of intimacy and welcome. The aisle carpet protects the unusually wide, heart-pine floors. The fine craftsmanship here was made possible by the fact that prosperous rice growers and cotton farmers had at their command a large force of skilled slave labor.

The wide center aisle is flanked by simple pews typical of the early nineteenth century. Natural light streams through the high, twelve-over-twelve sashed windows. The off-center window along the front wall is fairly atypical.
The gently curved ceiling rises above handsome crown molding, creating a cathedral-like effect within the sanctuary.

PHOTOGRAPHY BY GAIL DES JARDIN

Alpine Presbyterian

Alpine Presbyterian had its beginnings in Pleasant Grove in 1835 in a church named Enon. From this church, formed with fifteen members, the other Presbyterian churches in Chattooga County were later formed. Those Presbyterians in the neighborhood of Alpine worshipped in the upper room of a schoolhouse and met there once a month. Over time, the church prospered and the members resolved to build a new church and cemetery on land donated by Robert Boyles and Samuel Knox. A petition was then sent to the Presbytery of the Cherokee in March of 1853 asking for permission to form a church to be known as Alpine. The sanctuary was erected by John Henderson and Tom Allen with material donated by Samuel Knox in 1853. Few structural changes have been made since.

This seemingly peaceful place in the foothills of Northwest Georgia has seen much turmoil. The cemetery holds the remains of Hugh Montgomery, who was appointed by President Monroe in 1825 to be the Indian agent to the Cherokee nation. This part of Georgia was right in the middle of the Cherokee struggle to retain what was left of their lands. Gold had been discovered in North Georgia in 1828, and the Cherokee agent was repeatedly forced to deal with delicate situations on both sides. Montgomery remained in the position until the Cherokees were rounded up and marched west in 1838. The 1830 Indian Removal Act, passed by the U.S. Congress at the urging of President Andrew Jackson, resulted in the forced removal that became known as the infamous Trail of Tears.

The Cherokees in 1838 were the last to be evicted from their homelands in the southeastern states, following the Choctaws (1831), the Seminoles (1832), the Creeks (1834), and the Chickasaws (1837). By 1837, with staggering loss of life along the way, 46,000 Native Americans from this region alone had been marched west, thereby opening 25 million acres for predominantly white settlement. For his services, upon his retirement Hugh Lawson Montgomery was given a tract of 3,000 acres in Chattooga County, where he lived until his death in 1852.

In 1982 the church was reorganized under its present leadership and is now known as Alpine Community Church.

Although the sanctuary in Alpine is now outfitted with electricity, it projects largely the same impression as when the building was erected in 1853, with the possible exception of the blue ceiling. Daylight streams through high, nine-over-nine clear-glass windows to illuminate the almost circular chancel, partly nestled in the apse.

The view from the pulpit features the light and airy interior of this simple country church. The modest but intimate rear gallery provided a place of worship for slaves in the community.

Tucked between two windows overlooking the cemetery, this piano, made by the Bishop Piano Company of Rockford, Illinois, has served the congregation of Alpine for many years. The choir sits in the pews to the left.

The gallery brought its occupants, originally slaves but now overflow attendees, nearly to the altar. The spectacular natural light that floods the sanctuary is partly due to the siting of the church on the crown of a gentle slope.

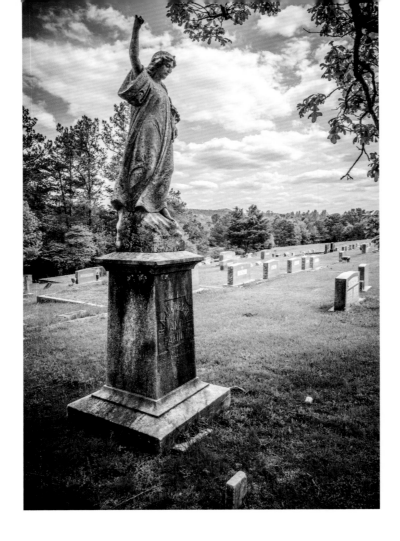

This angel with arm gesturing toward heaven presides over the graves of the McWhorter family. The first of the twenty-one McWhorters buried here was Margaret, who died in 1879.

Of the 757 interments in the cemetery, the best-known grave is that of Hugh Lawson Montgomery, who died in 1852, fourteen years after his job as the last Cherokee Indian agent ended with the forced removal of the Cherokees.

The church was positioned so that all the windows provide worshippers and visitors a rich and peaceful view of the Georgia foothills and the cemetery, which encircles the building.

PHOTOGRAPHY BY SCOTT MacINNIS

Fields Chapel United Methodist

Fields Chapel is, to a great extent, the story of Jeremiah Field and the Field family. It takes place at a seminal point in Georgia history involving vast amounts of cheap land, conflict with the Cherokee nation, the discovery of gold, and, ultimately, the tragic removal of the Cherokees. White encroachment on the land had begun by 1800 and was aided by what is now known as the old Federal Highway, which was laid across the northeast part of the county in 1805. The flow of settlers into the region became a flood after gold was discovered in 1828.

According to one church history, Fields Chapel was organized and the first structure built by Jeremiah Field sometime around 1820. However, a family document suggests he may have moved into Cherokee County at a later date. Regardless of the date, Jeremiah Field was one of the earliest settlers in Cherokee County; an entrepreneur, he owned a grist mill, a general store, and thousands of acres engaged in agriculture.

This original chapel remained in use until the present chapel was built by Charles Steele in 1898–1899. It was dedicated in June 1899 by the Reverend Samuel Porter Jones, with "3,000 people present . . . in spite of the rainy weather," according to the church history. At the time, Jones was arguably the most famous preacher in the country.

After its auspicious beginning, the little church prospered until the 1950s, when the community was threatened by the building of the Allatoona reservoir, which forced many residents to sell their land. So many people had relocated or had been simply cut off from access to the church that membership declined to a dozen or so. Fields Chapel has now fully rebounded and has an active United Methodist congregation.

As seen from the entrance of the 1899 meetinghouse, light streams
in through high, nine-over-nine windows along each wall and in the
apse. The roof features a trussed-rafter design.

The patterned panes, which became fashionable in
the late nineteenth century, provide colorful lighting
accents within the chapel. The original pews feature a
design seldom seen in rural churches, but the heart-pine
floors were common in the nineteenth century.

Dual entry doors were still common in Methodist churches of the era, even though segregated seating of men, women, and children was seldom practiced by then. When this meetinghouse was consecrated in 1899, the modern era was just around the corner. Gas or electric lighting (as seen here) was already becoming common. Some churches of this era even provided interior bathrooms.

Of the nearly two hundred recorded graves in the chapel
cemetery, twenty-two are of members of the Gramling
family. The first of the family to lie here (in foreground) was
Marthia E. Gramling, who died in 1895 at the age of sixteen.
In the background is the Field family burial ground. Among
the seventeen graves are those of founder Jeremiah Field
and his wife, Anna, both of whom died in 1857.

Dating from the time of the gold rush and the Cherokee Indian removal, this historic burial ground is nestled in a grove of trees in the Georgia foothills of Cherokee County.

Kiokee Baptist

Built in 1808, Kiokee Baptist is significant because of the longevity of the church, the long legacy of the Marshall family of preachers that served here, and the outstanding architecture of the structure. This is the third of seven buildings in which this congregation has worshipped.

The congregation began as a preaching point established by Daniel Marshall, the pastor of Stevens Creek (later renamed Big Stevens Creek) Baptist Church in South Carolina. In 1771 Daniel Marshall moved to Georgia and organized the church, which in keeping with Baptist tradition was named for a nearby geographical landmark, Kiokee Creek. This history earns Kiokee the distinction of being Georgia's oldest continuing Baptist congregation.

According to the *New Georgia Encyclopedia*, "From 1772 to 1792 the church met in the log cabin constructed by Daniel Marshall. This small building was similar to Quaker-style constructions of that era, probably twenty feet wide and twenty-four feet long. In 1792 a second building was constructed on the site, or near the site, of the original house of worship at Kiokee Creek. A more commodious brick building became the third church building at the same site in 1808, and it still stands."

The history of Kiokee is also unique in terms of the legacy of the founding pastor, Daniel Marshall (1706–1784), a Connecticut native, who ended a forty-two-year itinerant career at Kiokee, serving as its pastor for the last twelve years of his life. His son Abraham (1748–1819) was pastor when the 1808 meetinghouse was built, and he also served there until his death. Abraham was then succeeded by *his* son, Jabez (1795–1832), who repeated the now-established family business. Together, the Marshall men pastored the Kiokee flock for its first sixty-one years. They had a major impact on the growth of the Baptist Church in the early nineteenth century.

Finally, Kiokee Baptist is notable for its construction technique, quality, and architectural style. Although we know little of the specifics about the construction of Kiokee, it's possible to extrapolate what would have been required in 1808 to construct a church like this in the Georgia backcountry.

The skilled tradesmen who built this church could have been hired only by the wealthy planter class. Great wealth, stimulated by the use of the cotton gin invented by Eli Whitney in 1794, was beginning to be created in this part of Georgia in the early eighteenth century. Given the fertility of the Southeast Georgia soil, the number of slaves imported to work the land of the emerging plantation system, and the opening of huge tracts of cheap land as a result of the Cherokee and Creek land cessions, there were now fortunes to be made. King Cotton had arrived in the Georgia backcountry.

An unusual feature at this church is its three entrances. These rough
fieldstone steps leading to the primary entrance were placed in 1808.
Two centuries later, they still serve their original purpose well.

In the sanctuary, chamfered columns support a large gallery above. The handmade pews rest soundly on heart-pine floorboards. The walls are covered with plaster inside, and the exceptionally wide brick walls of the building create deep-set windows. This would have been the most striking building of any kind within miles. Today it is well maintained by the congregation of the Appling church nearby and is occasionally used for special church events.

Although not unheard of, a window behind the pulpit
is still unusual (see also Bark Camp, page 47). Here the
window is flanked by matching windows on either side,
seeming to evoke the Trinity.

The interior roof trusses and rafters are exceptionally strong. Giant interior cross beams sit atop thick brick walls. Twelve stout columns support the gallery and further protect the building and those within. The large, heavy doors can be barred from the inside, keeping an enemy out. Sitting alone on the frontier, Kiokee and other early rural churches were places of not just spiritual refuge but physical refuge, as well. Congregants and village dwellers could flee to the church for safety when threatened by outlaws, enemy soldiers, storms, and other dangers. They often did.

This stone stands over the grave of Abraham Marshall, the second Marshall to minister to the congregation.

The floors and doors are all made of heart-pine lumber. The trees would have been several hundred years old when they were harvested and planed in the late eighteenth or early nineteenth century for these doors. The hinges still function as well today as they did when first hammered into shape around 1808 when Thomas Jefferson was just ending his second term.

OPPOSITE: We managed to haul this original pew into the light at one of the side entrances so you could see and appreciate the craftsmanship and joinery that went into its making. Mortises and tenons joined wide, single boards of varying thickness to create these pews.

Jerusalem Lutheran

Standing above the Savannah River some thirty miles north of its mouth, the Jerusalem Evangelical Lutheran Church is the oldest church building in Georgia. It is sometimes referred to as the oldest public building in the state.

The church was organized by a group of European settlers known as the Salzburgers, Protestants who made their way to Effingham County after the Catholic archbishop expelled them from the nation-state of Salzburg (in present-day Austria) in 1731. These religious refugees organized their church in 1733 in Augsburg (in present-day Germany), where they found support and encouragement that led them to England, and from there to the New World.

The church's pastors, John Martin Bolzius and Israel Christian Gronau, landed at Savannah in March 1734 with the first group of Protestant refugees. The German-speaking congregation originally settled along Ebenezer Creek, as instructed by Georgia founder James Oglethorpe. After this remote site produced further hardships, they were given permission a few years later to relocate along the Savannah River. They established New Ebenezer in 1797. As the original settlement at Ebenezer gradually disappeared into wilderness, New Ebenezer became known simply as Ebenezer.

The Salzburgers were wealthy, industrious people, and the church's architecture and construction reflect this. The oldest rural brick church in the state, Jerusalem Lutheran was built between 1767 and 1769 of bricks handmade of local clay.

The town of Ebenezer proved unable to recover from the severe damage it sustained during the Revolutionary War. Briefly the capital of Georgia, and then the county seat, it continued to lose businesses and residents over the years.

Remarkably, this church has remained active for more than a century after the town of Ebenezer virtually vanished. Today it still has an active congregation and is the oldest continuing Lutheran congregation in the United States worshipping in the same building. The church was placed on the National Register of Historic Places in 1974.

The sprightliness and functionality of the sanctuary belie the church's age.
The deeply recessed lower-level windows topped by smaller, clear second-
story windows have shed swaths of light into the sanctuary since 1769.

Unlike many rural churches, Jerusalem has remained active and occupied, well loved and well attended throughout its history. The lively banners, posted hymns, and choral binders are evidence of an active congregation at Jerusalem Evangelical Lutheran. This continuity is even more remarkable given that its hometown has essentially vanished.

The architectural design and construction of this church were much
more sophisticated than those of other early rural Georgia churches.
The slave gallery is commodious, and its chamfered columns with Doric
capitols make quite a statement. The stained gallery rail provides a pleasing
contrast to the walls and ceiling. The painted pews with walnut scrolled
endcaps are unique to this era.

The entry gate to the Jerusalem Cemetery is
handsome and grand: a soaring, Victorian, brick
Roman arch bounded by two highly decorative curved
walls. This late nineteenth-century arch was added a
hundred or so years after the church's completion.

Because of its early founding date and its continuous use, this cemetery contains burials from the mid-eighteenth century to today—quite rare, if not unique, in Georgia. Some of the original, unmarked graves of the 1700s are now identifiable only by the depressions in the ground that developed with the disintegration of the coffin. Other primitive early graves are marked by simple, uninscribed fieldstones.

One of the early pastors of Jerusalem, the Reverend John E. Bergmann served the church from 1788 to his death in 1824. Also buried on the grounds are the founders of the congregation, the Reverends John Martin Bolzius (1703–1765) and Israel Christian Gronau (?–1745).

PHOTOGRAPHY BY GAIL DES JARDIN

Sardis Presbyterian

FLOYD COUNTY   ORG. 1836

Fifteen years before this church was established, the first missionaries were dispatched to this part of Georgia to minister to the Cherokees. Their residence was located on this site just north of the cemetery wall. The mission they established, Turnip Mountain Mission, also known as Haweis, was 2 miles to the east. Sardis Presbyterian Church was organized in November 1836, two years before the Cherokees were marched away. A plank-sheathed log church served the congregation until it built the present church in 1855, slightly south of the original structure.

During the Civil War throughout the South, companies and smaller units of the new Confederate States Army were often made up of men from the same locale. The Sixth Georgia Cavalry was formed by a group of Sardis Volunteers that organized on the grounds of the church in May 1861. Brothers Major Alfred Bale and Lieutenant Charles Bale are among the eighteen Confederate soldiers buried in the cemetery.

After the war, the congregation undertook several changes, including the founding of a Sunday school in 1877. However, at this time, membership began to decline from its high of 173. By 1907, fewer than three dozen members remained. In 1979 the church officially dissolved, although the building was opened for sporadic services in later years and occasional repairs were performed. Fortunately, local residents banded together to save the property, and in 1990 it was deeded to the Sardis Preservation Society, earning a place on the National Register of Historic Places in January 2005.

Even accounting for reversing the pews and pulpit in 1877, the interior has changed little
since the church was built in 1855, due partly to the efforts of the Sardis Preservation Society.
The pews, wide-board walls, and unusual board-and-batten ceiling remain intact, and much of
the lighting within appears to be electrified, old oil-burning lamps.

The handmade pews, nine-over-nine windows, and wide horizontal wallboards are evidence of the "modest-and-simple" rule followed by the founders of this Presbyterian congregation. The new settlers in this part of Georgia were predominantly Scots-Irish who immigrated into Georgia from the highlands of South and North Carolina after the Revolutionary War.

The view from the pulpit is of an exceedingly utilitarian, even plain, worship space. Unlike Baptist churches, here there is no dividing wall or line to separate the men from the women and children. Rather than serving to divide the congregation by gender, the dual entrances align with the side aisles to expedite access.

Probably replacing a modest piano in the late nineteenth century, this expensive (for the period) Mason and Hamlin organ/harmonium is evidence of the congregation's having grown in size as well as in its fortunes since the church's modest beginnings.

Although the original pine flooring has been replaced with narrow oak floor boards, the remaining mid-nineteenth-century wooden elements are sound and solid, including this stout pulpit. The twin pulpit lamps were originally oil burners but have been converted to electric.

The oldest of the 253 recorded interments in the graveyard is that of the Reverend James McArver, who died in 1841. The most recent burial was in 1984. Eighteen Confederate Civil War soldiers also lie here.

These imposing but elegant twin markers stand over the Civil War graves of the Bale brothers, who served in the Sixth Georgia Cavalry. Major Alfred Bale fell at the age of twenty-four in 1863 near Dandridge, Tennessee, in the December fighting over control of Knoxville, and twenty-six-year-old Lieutenant Charles Bale was killed five months later in the Battle of Resaca in Georgia.

Carroll's Methodist

A 1950s exterior remodel of Carroll's Methodist Church that added siding, a portico, and bannisters gives little indication that this structure dates to 1833. Like many rural churches of its era, the church was built without a foundation, but the church's original footings and support beams were covered in the 1950s and the doors and several windows were redesigned. While adding decades of life to the church, these well-meaning efforts significantly altered its historical character. Fortunately, the primitive beauty of Carroll's is largely preserved in the interior.

The church's earliest history states that it was founded in 1797, during the beginning years of Methodism in Georgia and the United States. It was named for the William Carroll family, early settlers in Franklin County. A November 22, 1799, entry in the diary of Methodist bishop Francis Asbury describes his having preached at this church in its original structure: "We came sixteen miles to Carroll's Meeting House; a new log cabin in the woods. Some of the people of the congregation are from the east and west parts of Maryland. I felt the Lord was with them. We have the kitchen, house, and chamber all in one, and no closet [bathroom] but the woods."

Asbury is credited with helping to establish Methodism in the state. Born in England, he had been appointed by one of the founders of Methodism, John Wesley, as a traveling preacher. Immigrating to the United States while still a young man, Asbury vastly expanded his itinerant ministry, preaching and lecturing as he rode around the country. The Second Great Awakening in Georgia and elsewhere in the South helped his words take root, and by the start of the Civil War, Methodist membership had increased nearly 1,000 percent in fewer than fifty years.

The location of the woodstove near the pulpit might have
encouraged congregants to take seats near the front of the church on
rainy, cold winter days. Apart from the electric lights and ceiling fans,
the view today is much as it would have been for the well-known
and respected Reverend Nelson Osborn, who in the mid-nineteenth
century conducted nearly five hundred funerals and even more
marriage ceremonies here.

The pews are sawn and hand planed from local heart-pine boards, then joined by the mortise and tenon technique. The lap blankets on these pews near the rear of the sanctuary speak eloquently to the lack of central heating then and now.

Although the heart-pine floors throughout the church are original, the Gothic doors
and the altar were added in the mid-1950s, when other minor interior modifications
were also made. The pump organ was a late nineteenth-century addition.

Opposite the pump organ behind the pulpit stands a
Victorian-era piano, suggesting that the Carroll's Methodists
are a singing congregation.

The original windows and doors were severely cut down in the 1950s to remake them in Gothic style. The resulting repairs to the interior walls reveal the approximate original dimensions. Thankfully, the mid-twentieth-century compulsion to renovate has given way to a deeper appreciation of and respect for historic architecture. Today, the authenticity of this 1833 structure prevails.

John Adam Miller rests beside his wife, Nancy Casey Miller. They were married in January 1854 in this church and had seven children in all. Having served with both the Ninth and the Thirty-Seventh Georgia Infantries, John returned from the Civil War to sire the last four children with his wife. Near to this grave lie John's parents, Uriah and Sarah Miller.

Bethesda Baptist

Large, federal-style brick churches were not typical in the late eighteenth-century South, which makes Bethesda Baptist Church unusual and particularly so because of its rural location. One of the oldest brick churches in Georgia, it is a bricks-and-mortar embodiment of the wealth early white settlers were accruing in this part of Georgia. The only other known brick churches in rural Georgia built prior to 1820 are Kiokee Baptist, built in 1808 (see 79), and Jerusalem Lutheran, built in 1769 (see 89).

The congregation was organized in 1785 as Whatley's Mill Church in what was then Washington County, which in 1786 was redistricted into the newly formed Greene County. Georgia was expanding rapidly after the 1783 Treaty of Paris, and the larger counties were being subdivided as a result.

The owner of a local grist mill, Samuel Whatley, donated the land where the church now stands, and the congregation is believed to have worshipped in the mill in its earliest days. Although the current sanctuary was completed in November 1818, construction probably began a few years earlier since the bricks were handmade on the premises from local clay. Also in 1818, the name was changed to "Baptist Church at Bethesda" by an act of incorporation by the Georgia General Assembly. The first pastor was the well-known Jesse Mercer.

According to Richard Noegel's *A History of Bethesda Baptist Church*, "during slavery days, slaves were members of their owners' congregations. They attended services with their masters and sat in a gallery above the main floor. This was true in churches of all denominations throughout the slave states." Only after slavery ended did segregated services become the norm. In 1834, "at the congregation's regular conference. Bethesda's black members asked for permission to have 'Brother Sam. a man of colour' to 'attend them and preach for them once a month at this place.'" In spite of recent fears that included the 1831 slave insurrection led by Nat Turner in Virginia, permission was granted, "allowing Brother Sam to preach to the black congregation on the second Sabbath in each month. . . . However, on June 18, 1836, the church withdrew permission for the slaves to use the meeting house any further because of 'some disorder.'"

Since 1850, the church building has undergone major structural changes, improvements, and the expected modernizations necessary to stay current. The Bethesda Baptist congregation is still active and strong. Care and maintenance of the building shows evidence of a caring and devoted membership.

The stout walls and doors, soaring ceiling, illumination from many suspended oil lamps (now converted to electric), and the natural light from large windows have created an inviting worship environment within this sanctuary for two centuries.

From the gallery, the grandeur of the sanctuary and the unique
clerestory designed in 1815 are more apparent. The structural
remains of the gallery removed in about 1850 are visible below
the clerestory windows along the right wall.

Church records show that most of the glass in the windows
dates to 1850—until that time, only closing the shutters
protected the interior from the weather. The pews probably also
date from the 1850 remodel. Visible through this window is the
cemetery, begun in 1888 and populated by prominent Greene
County citizens. Particularly well represented is the Thornton
family that had settled nearby Thornton Crossroads, which
later became Union Point.

The congregation still treasures many relics of its past, including its records back to 1817 (earlier records have been lost) along with this handmade wooden bench dating from the church's early days.

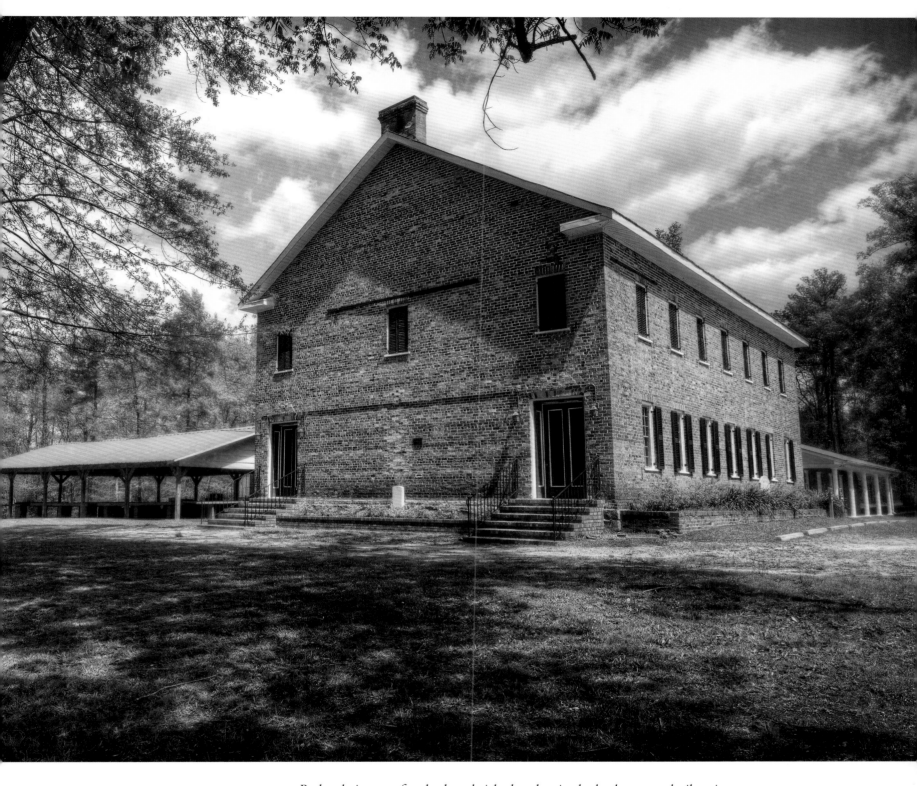

Bethesda is one of only three brick churches in the backcountry built prior to 1820. Unlike the plentiful and readily available wood, the bricks were formed and fired, probably by slaves, from local clay in what must have seemed an interminable process, given the numbers necessary for this substantial structure. That Bethesda Baptist stands so strong today is a testament to the slave labor that built it and to the dedication of later generations in preserving it.

Penfield Baptist

Penfield Baptist was designed by David Demorest and built in 1846 as the
Mercer University Chapel for the then princely sum of $6,794. This striking
Greek revival brick building commands a grassy hill in the quiet community
of Penfield, which was named for Deacon Josiah Penfield, an early benefactor
of Mercer. Established as a manual-labor school, Mercer prospered in
Penfield after its opening in 1833, developing into one of the state's most
prominent learning institutions as well as a seat of the Baptist movement
in Georgia.

Nine years after the Georgia Baptist Convention voted in 1871 to move
the university to the larger and more active city of Macon, the university
deeded its Penfield properties to the Georgia Baptist Convention. They, in
turn, deeded Mercer Chapel to Penfield Baptist, which had been meeting
in the building since 1839.

A century later, the Penfield congregation surrendered its church
because of financial difficulties, and Mercer University again found itself in
possession of the building, which was by then in steep decline. However, the
late twentieth-century renaissance of appreciation for heritage and historic
structures led to the complete restoration of Mercer Chapel by a group of
supporters, who then returned it to the Penfield Baptist Church. It is now
part of Penfield Historic District.

A welcoming atmosphere greets visitors as they come through
the main entrance. The rear balcony lowers the entryway ceiling,
providing an intimate spot from which to contemplate the soaring
space of the nave. Unimpeded views and the white, elevated
chancel beckon you to enter.

OPPOSITE: This graceful chapel now looks much as it did
when the structure was new in 1846, thanks to a careful and
thoughtful restoration that preserved the heart-pine floors,
pews, galleries, and stately columns.

Penfield's classical interior is rare among rural Georgia churches. The full-height Doric columns at the rear appear to raise the ceiling higher, and additional columns support the balconies along the two sides. The 48-over-48 double-hung windows admit ample illumination into the nave. The old-style pews retain the center partition that originally separated men and women.

A respectful nod to the building's history is found in this permanent display: an original issue of the *Christian Index*, a Southern Baptist publication that was printed on the Mercer campus from 1840 to 1857. It was founded by John Boswell and listed the Reverend Jesse Mercer as a contributor and supporter.

As seen in this close-up of the chancel, the restoration overseers made a conscious decision to minimize the visible intrusion of twenty-first-century technology in the clear, uncluttered lines of the sanctuary. The marriage of preservation and modernization makes this rural church a gracious and well-equipped home for a twenty-first-century congregation.

This photograph speaks both to the authenticity of the restoration and to the continued vibrancy of the church as it approaches its bicentennial.

PHOTOGRAPHY BY RANDY CLEGG

Grace-Calvary Episcopal

HABERSHAM COUNTY   ORG. 1838

In 1838, the state's sixth Episcopal parish was established in the Blue Ridge foothills community of Clarkesville as Grace Protestant Episcopal Church, and the following year the congregation began building this Greek Revival sanctuary. The history of the church is closely tied to the development of the area as a summer escape for well-to-do Georgians seeking relief from the sweltering and disease-ridden lowland counties.

Cherokee cessions in July 1817 and February 1819 led to the creation of Habersham County in 1818, and Clarkesville was designated the county seat in 1823. After gold was discovered in the nearby Nacoochee Valley in 1828, white pressure to settle there increased, resulting in the forcible removal of the Cherokees in 1838.

That same year, Clarkesville's Episcopalian summer residents established Grace Episcopal as a mission church, holding services in a nearby Methodist church. In 1839 the church purchased a lot to construct its own worship space. The architect of the church was a cousin of President Martin Van Buren, Jarvis Van Buren, who came from New York to Clarkesville in 1838 to manage the Stroop Iron Works and to work as a railroad engineer. Although construction began in 1839, a local drought and some lawsuits caused delays. As a result, the sanctuary was not finished and consecrated until 1842, by which time the church had been granted parish status.

The membership of Grace Episcopal declined after the Civil War, and the church eventually lost its parish status. In 1971 it joined with Calvary Episcopal, a mission church in the more substantial and year-round town of Cornelia. In 1972, Grace-Calvary received parish status once again and undertook the difficult task of restoring the nineteenth-century structure, which had deteriorated so far as to be condemned. Since then, the congregation has continued to improve the building and to make careful renovations to honor this historic church. The organ, a cherished relic dating to 1848, and the bell, cast in Massachusetts in 1852, remain operational. The church was added to the National Register of Historic Places in 1980.

Lying a few blocks from Grace-Calvary, Old Clarkesville Cemetery dates to 1831 and is on the site of the town's first Methodist church, now gone. Both Grace-Calvary and the cemetery are part of the Washington-Jefferson Street Historic District.

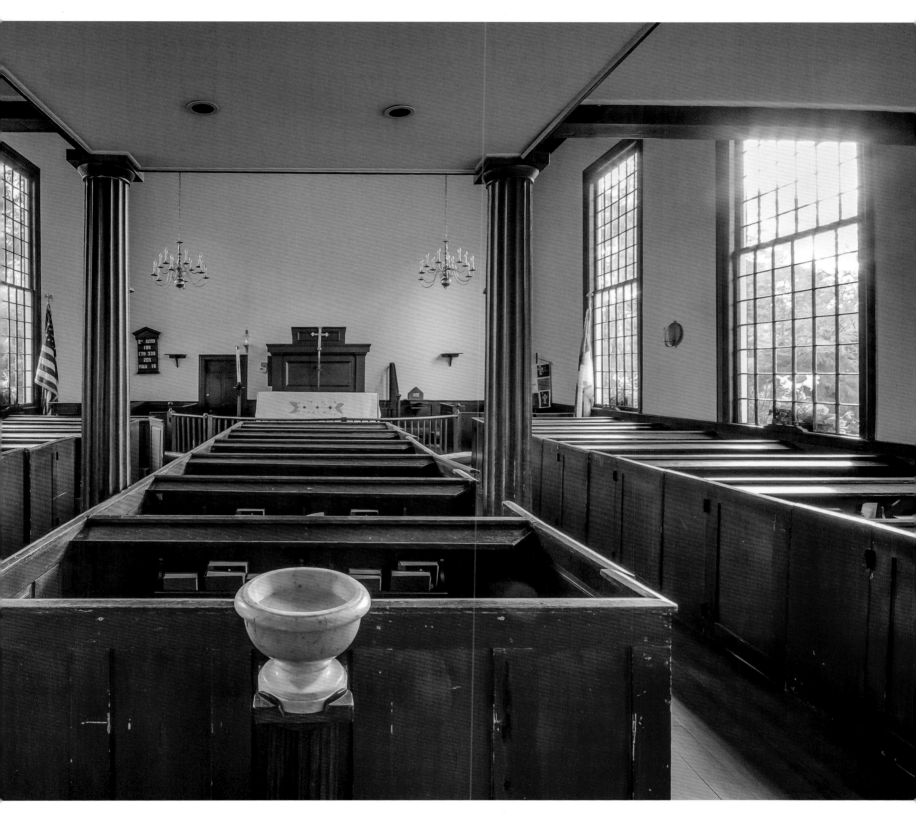

This 1842 church underwent a massive restoration inside and out in the 1970s to stabilize the structure. Changes since then have also been careful to preserve the historic integrity of the original design, so this view from the back of the sanctuary is not substantially different from what it was in the nineteenth century.

The enormous 42-over-42 windows with hand-floated panes reflect the taste and architectural expertise of Jarvis Van Buren. The large, heavy pews were expensive to build because of the amount of wood and hardware; these twenty-first-century reproductions of the commodious and dominating originals faithfully reflect the social stature and prosperity of the wealthy Low Country families who occupied them during their summer sojourn.

Tall windows preserve the exterior architectural symmetry but also illuminate the slave gallery within. The dip in the middle of the gallery was constructed to accommodate the unexpected height of the organ. The angled cutouts above the pews on either side at the rear of the sanctuary accommodate the staircases leading from the narthex to the gallery.

Grace Episcopal may have Georgia's oldest
working pipe organ, fabricated of black walnut
in 1848 by the nationally respected Henry Erben.
When delivered from New York and assembled
on-site, the organ was discovered to be too tall,
so the resourceful congregation reconfigured the
gallery to accommodate it. Restored in the latter
twentieth century, this organ still accompanies
the congregation.

After the church passed its sesquicentennial, reproduction pews and altar desks were placed on the chancel, restoring the original 1848 configuration. The tapestries on the curved altar kneelers depict the Blue Ridge foothills surrounding Clarkesville.

Jarvis Van Buren is buried in Old Clarkesville Cemetery, just a few
blocks away from where he built Grace Episcopal. His talents as a master
architect are obvious in the beauty of Grace Episcopal. Van Buren also
designed residences and other churches in the area.

The obelisk in the foreground marks the final resting place in Old Clarkesville
Cemetery of Camillus P. Wyly, who died in the Battle of Fredericksburg on December
18, 1862. Beside him is the grave of his grandfather, General James Rutherford Wyly,
a veteran of the War of 1812 and a prominent citizen of Georgia.

Powelton Baptist

According to R. L. Robinson's *History of the Georgia Baptist Association*, this meetinghouse was built in 1798, making it the oldest existing Baptist church building in the state. It also speaks to the growing importance of the village of Powelton at the end of the eighteenth century (see more about Powelton in the next entry, Powelton Methodist).

In July 1786, a group of twenty-six people, including the Reverend Silas Mercer, organized the congregation as Powell's Creek Church. Silas had founded several of the earliest Baptist Churches, most notably Phillips Mill, where he served as pastor until succeeded by his son, Jesse Mercer, in February 1797. Mercer University, now located in Macon, is named in honor of Jesse, who served as pastor at Powelton Baptist for twenty-eight years.

It would be difficult to overstate the importance of Silas Mercer, Jesse Mercer, and the Powelton Baptist Church to the growth and success of the Baptist denomination in post–Revolutionary War Georgia. The lack of central authority and the freedom held by individual churches in the Baptist denomination particularly appealed to those who had just successfully rejected the yoke of British control. Consequently, in the decade from 1780 to 1790, the number of Baptists in Georgia ballooned from 261 to 3,355— with most of the growth occurring in the years just after the war.

Powelton was the site of many historic meetings as the Baptists continued to aggressively recruit members and began to address the challenges of governance. In 1803, the General Committee of the Georgia Baptists, a forerunner of the state convention, was organized during meetings held at Powelton Baptist Church. The Georgia Baptist

Convention was held here in 1822, 1823, and 1832. Georgia governor William Rabun was a member and the choral master of the church.

The current meetinghouse was remodeled by adding Sunday school rooms to the original 1798 structure in the early twentieth century. A bell tower and covered porch were added in 1822, probably before the first Georgia Baptist Convention. Other modifications were made over the years. Membership peaked in the early 1800s at 250, but Powelton Baptist remains an active church, as it has been for over two hundred years.

This sanctuary dates back to 1798, with later additions springing up around it. The interior of the church is spartan even today, as would be expected of a structure built of local materials in the late eighteenth century. The structural members and floors were all cut and hand planed from the giant pine trees present on or near the site. At the rear of the sanctuary, two rooms were added during remodeling in the early twentieth century.

The pews are original. The subtle notches running down the middle of the backs of the center pews accommodated the railing that originally separated the congregants, men to the left, women and children to the right. This separation also extended to the original entry doors of the sanctuary.

The 1798 structure consisted of a rectangular sanctuary alone. In the photo, that initial structure is represented by the larger center gable. Forward of, and to the left and right of that sanctuary gable, we see additions that were made in the early twentieth century. Other additions not visible in the photo include school rooms projecting from the sides of the original church building as well as a rectangular addition to the east wall that provided an expanded chancel-pulpit area and apse. The memorial within the enclosure in the foreground is to William Rabun, who died in Powelton while still governor.

In a wooded hollow across the road is this spring-fed baptismal pool that we are told has been in use since the church was formed in 1786. Baptism by immersion remains one of the basic tenants of many southern Baptist churches.

PHOTOGRAPHY BY SCOTT FARRAR

Powelton Methodist

One of the oldest villages in the state, Powelton was an important town in the post–Revolutionary War Georgia backcountry. When Hancock County was formed in 1795, Powelton was already home to prominent citizens, thriving merchant and commercial enterprises, and academies of higher education for both men and women. It was also a major crossroads community in early nineteenth-century Georgia. The story goes that Powelton rivaled Milledgeville for the location of the new state capital after Louisville's turn but came up two votes short. A Methodist history of the Powelton church dated 1951 in the Augusta district of the Northern Conference also mentions the "two votes short" story.

Little history of the Methodist church at Powelton is available, but some evidence indicates that the church was organized prior to 1800. Powelton Baptist Church, a short distance away, was consecrated in 1786, and New Smyrna Methodist, ten miles away, was organized in 1790. The earliest documented grave in the cemetery is dated 1817. However, a 1972 document in the Emory University archives mentions graves with dates of 1802 and 1803. Some recent Methodist records in the District Archives place the construction date of the present sanctuary as 1830. The 1972 "History of the Powelton, Ga. Methodist Church" at Pitts Theology Library states that the present building replaced an earlier "Methodist meetinghouse."

The cemetery age and location support the supposition that the current building was built on the site of the first sanctuary. Despite the age of the footings and timbers, the interior of the church remains level and stable. In 1946 it was "completely repaired, recovered, and repainted," according to the 1951 Methodist history. The church has been inactive since the 1970s. A few local residents maintain the cemetery and the structure to some degree, although the church is badly in need of further support.

The view from the pulpit reveals a beautiful example of the vernacular for an early nineteenth-century rural church. In 2009, location scouts for the motion picture *Get Low* (starring Robert Duvall, Sissy Spacek, and Bill Murray) came across this church and declared it perfect for a brief scene in the film. The producers spent a small amount of money to bring the interior up to movie standards, but since filming the compromised exterior has again wrought damage inside.

Rural craftsmanship is evident in the handmade, unadorned pews resting on wide, heart-pine floorboards. Wide horizontal wallboards stack to meet three- and four-inch ceiling boards. The clear glass in the nine-over-nine windows illuminates the 1830s chancel and apse framed by an arch. The woodstove would have made the sanctuary habitable on cold winter mornings.

The lack of maintenance has made the structure vulnerable to the elements. Vines and trees have invaded through broken windows and the clapboard siding is compromised, wreaking havoc within. Weather intrusion has virtually destroyed the piano.

OPPOSITE: The clean lines and beauty of the sanctuary still invoke a sense of calm, even decades after the building last served as a place of worship.

153

The Confederate gravestone in the left foreground is that of author Sonny Seals's great-grandfather, William D. Seals. In July 1861, William D. enlisted in Company K, Fifteenth Georgia Infantry. Four years later, he returned to Powelton and the family farm after being wounded at the Battle of the Wilderness. For more of the story, see the preface (page xiv).

Although structures of this size and age were generally
supported with unmortared fieldstones piled into pillars,
Powelton Methodist features rough, single-fieldstone
vertical footings. That this church remains plumb and level
is a tribute to the circa-1830 builders.

PHOTOGRAPHY BY SCOTT FARRAR

St. Paul CME

The history of St. Paul CME (Colored Methodist Episcopal) Church cannot
be told without relating the story of the renowned farmer and plantation owner
David Dickson. He was one of the wealthiest planters in Hancock County at a time
when it was arguably the wealthiest county in pre–Civil War Georgia. Even though
his land was not regarded as particularly suited to raising cotton or other cash crops,
Dickson pioneered agricultural techniques that were far ahead of his time.

Although well respected in life, Dickson caused an uproar among the region's
white planters upon his death in 1885, when his will revealed that he had named as
his sole heir his daughter, Amanda, by a family slave, Julia. Then in her midthirties,
Amanda was set to inherit all of Dickson's landholdings—about 17,000 acres
appraised at $309,000, a fortune at the time. After battling legally with the other
Dickson would-be heirs all the way to the Georgia Supreme Court, Amanda
America Dickson won her right to her father's land, becoming the wealthiest
African American woman in the nation.

The St. Paul CME Church was organized in 1857 in a brush arbor by slaves on
the Dickson Plantation. This in itself makes it unusual, because few blacks had
organized their own churches prior to the Civil War. After the war, in 1870, Dickson
deeded property over to the church near the brush arbor where services had been
conducted. This property is now the site of the original church, which was built, we
are told, between 1870 and 1877. The old sanctuary sits on high ground overlooking
the former lands of the Dickson plantation. We are told that it was also near many

of the old plantation slave houses, all of which are now gone. The congregation remains active today, having established a new sanctuary about two miles from the historic building depicted here. The peacefulness of the church grounds invites reflection on the lives of slaves and former slaves as they struggled to define themselves within the limits of their reality. Today the descendants of the Dickson plantation slaves meet for an annual reunion to celebrate their heritage and the history of the old church.

The simple and traditional design of the typical rural church is modified by the single tower in a front corner. The tower is the dominant architectural feature and still contains the original church bell that announced the services to the former slaves and their children residing close by.

According to Harrell Lawson's *History of St. Paul CME Church*,
"This property also contains a building previously used as a
school for the secular education of the youth of the community
and as a meeting place for Masons and a burial society founded
by St. Paul members in the early 1900's." We estimate the
construction date to have been sometime prior to 1910.

This view of the still-active St. Paul cemetery perfectly reflects its African American roots. Marble, granite, and concrete stone monuments from different eras stand alongside each other in no apparent order. The old schoolhouse and Masonic hall are visible behind the church at far right. The low building alongside the church was a much later addition.

PHOTOGRAPHY BY SCOTT MacINNIS

Apple Valley Baptist

This old structure is in a lovely rural setting, on the crest of a gently sloping hill that commands a 360-degree view of the beautiful Jackson County countryside. Documents in the Baptist archives at the Georgia State Convention state that Apple Valley Baptist was organized May 7, 1887, in a school building with thirty-four charter members and that the church was built in 1888. A local history tells that before the church was organized in 1887, Baptists in the community attended church services at Cabin Creek, Black's Creek, and Oconee Baptist. There is also local history that tells us this building was used as a schoolhouse in the early twentieth century before being abandoned.

The 1887 date is consistent with the age of the building seen here. It has a classic rural box construction with four windows along each of the two sides and a double-door entry on the end; there is no steeple. Deserted for some time, the structure is now being used as a stable and for farm storage. The tin roof remains in good shape and speaks to the beauty and longevity of tin as a perfect roofing material for these old backcountry sanctuaries. The structure is fairly sound, given the long period of total neglect and the pressure of the animals housed within. The quaint old cemetery across the road is worthy of attention, as well.

It is doubtful this structure was ever painted, as there remain
no signs of paint on it now. The side windows are boarded up
but probably matched this one on the end. You are looking at
the original glass in a four-over-twelve configuration, which
is rare, as is the horse standing in the lee of church. As a
testimony to the dilapidated condition of the structure, we see
the remains of a single vertical pilaster that once supported a
roof above the now-nonexistent porch.

Given what the Bible says about where Christ was born, there is something poetic about a church being used as a stable. The cutaway detail here reveals the hand-hewn timbers supported by stuccoed brick pillars as well as framing timbers and attractive lap siding on the interior walls. The horses grazing in the distance enter the building through a door cut into the wall where the altar was.

Even with the gaping hole at the back of the building, the structure is in remarkably good condition. With the church sited on the knoll of this hill, light would have flooded the sanctuary through the original twelve large windows on all four sides.

W. J. C. Hunt survived the Civil War, only to be struck down at the age of sixty-two in a farm accident. According to his *Jackson Herald* obituary in 1898, as "the mules trotted down a hill, he got over balanced and fell from the top of the cotton to the ground, breaking his collar bone and cracking his skull bone, producing death in a few hours."

This cemetery contains the remains of many generations of Apple Valley volunteers who answered the call of duty to their country throughout its struggles: Revolutionary War veterans, Civil War veterans, World War II survivors of the Bataan death march, and others lie together on this peaceful hillside.

PHOTOGRAPHY BY SCOTT MacINNIS

Thyatira Presbyterian

Although many Presbyterian churches in South Georgia are located in more urban areas and have a feeling of understated wealth about them, in these northern counties Presbyterian churches tend to be in more rural locations and of more primitive design and construction. Such is the case with Thyatira, founded in the rolling hills of Jackson County by Scots-Irish revolutionary soldiers who came here because of the cheap land and stayed to wrest a living out of the wilderness.

The church was founded around 1795 as the Olney Presbyterian Church at the Hurricane Shoals settlement, which had been started by James Montgomery, a Revolutionary War soldier. The church was formed with forty-two people on the west side of the shoals in a two-room building. According to the *Jackson Herald*, the church got its name because the congregation sang Olney hymns, from the Olney-Buckinghamshire Parish in England, rather than the traditional music from the psalms.

In 1828, the Thyatira Presbyterian Church of Rowan County, North Carolina, recognized the Jackson County church for its works and served as its sponsor, thus the name Thyatira. In 1830 land was deeded to the church elders, and the church was built on its present site. The building consists of several sections from different eras. Its unpretentiousness reflects the work ethic and the no-nonsense approach to spiritual matters on the part of the old Scots-Irish founders.

This classic example of a Georgia backcountry church exhibits no frills and was handmade from materials available locally. With the exception of the fine pews, the workmanship is entirely functional. The fact that uniformly wide boards were used for the walls and ceiling reflects the builders' frugality and functional focus. The patched ceiling to the right of the fan near the altar suggests where the flue for the woodstove exited through the roof.

The large, rather plain cross behind the altar immediately draws the eye down the wide center aisle, up the slightly raised podium, and past the three high-back chairs. The pine floors are adorned only with their natural patina.

A look into the crawl space beneath the church confirms this is a very old, hand-built structure. The hand-hewn support beams are joined with rounded or half-rounded logs, indicating early, unsophisticated construction techniques. Rather than saw marks, we saw only evidence of adzes, framing hatchets, wood chisels, and hand planes put to work.

OPPOSITE: The blinds in the window attest to modern use of the sanctuary. Although uncushioned, the well-worn pews still manage to look inviting. The cemetery on a small rise is visible through the six-over-six clear-glass windows.

The three chairs behind the altar represent the Trinity: Father, Son, and Holy Ghost. The large cross with a single central medallion dominates this sanctuary. The carpeting is the only embellishment on the otherwise simple, slightly raised chancel.

Sixteen Burnses are interred here in the family plot. In the foreground lie General David M. Burns and his children. We are not sure of the origin of the title of general: born in 1790 and deceased in 1864, David Burns did not serve in the Revolutionary War, and he would have been too old for Civil War service. Lying not here, but in Indianapolis, is one of his sons (Alonzo Waddle Burns), who died at the age of eighteen while serving in the Georgia Sixteenth Cavalry in the Civil War.

Concord Primitive Baptist

The available records disagree about the founding of Concord Primitive Baptist. One record states the church was founded in 1815 when 2 acres of land were transferred to the church by George Morris. Another record states the church was founded in October 1808. Partial church minutes dating back to 1812 have been preserved at Mercer University, suggesting that the 1808 date is correct.

Although historic church minutes are often mundane and repetitive, occasionally they come alive with insight into the lives and concerns of the early Georgia pioneers.

October 21, 1820: "A charge brought in by brother Lowry against brother Williams for making use of unchristian language to his wife and for his contradicting her and saying she had not discharged her duty as a wife and likewise for charging brother Lowry for saying that brother Williams had told a palpable lye. And for saying brother Lowry had told a Lye and he could prove it, the above charges laid over to the next Conference."

March 24, 1821: "Brother Absolom Achols came forward with an acknowledgment for drinking to much Spirits. the brethren feel to forgive him."

June 22, 1821: "Excommunicated Absalom Echols for the sin of drunkenesss [sic]."

What strikes us most about old minutes like these is the church's role in just about every facet of life in these early times. The church was community center, moderator, dating service, social services, courthouse with judge and jury, and whatever else the community needed to function as a civilized society. The church could be forgiving, but the ultimate punishment was excommunication after a peer review of the transgression. Excommunication at this time was not a punishment rooted in theology—it was a sentence that branded you as a social pariah and banished you from the comforts of church and community.

Nothing in this photograph suggests it was taken in the twenty-first century other than the tin roof that has replaced original wood shingles. It stands as it always has, a simple church where the elders tried to comfort and govern the community, far from any vestiges of what we think of as civilization.

Without the materials available locally to make mortar for a
foundation in remote early nineteenth-century locations,
a common technique was to create footings of stacked stones.
These have supported the substantial Concord Primitive
Baptist for two centuries.

Despite the utilitarian construction and unadorned interior, the quiet dignity of the
sanctuary is undeniable. The fuse box on the back wall shows the short-lived intrusion
of modernity. Some believe that the present pews were not original but borrowed
for use from a local train depot passenger waiting room. Given the community's
hardscrabble existence, that could have been the case.

These two-hundred-year-old floor joists were hand planed
and hewn flat on top but left rounded on the bottom with
the bark still intact. Concord Baptist is among the oldest
standing churches in the Georgia backcountry.

Of the thirty-four documented graves in this cemetery, the McDowell
clan claims the greatest number. As usual in cemeteries this old, there are a
number of unmarked graves lost to the ravages of time, which is a hindrance
to those seeking their own roots or local history.

Big Buckhead Baptist

Big Buckhead Church, the third oldest Baptist church in Georgia, was organized in 1774 and named for nearby Buckhead Creek. Completed and dedicated in 1855, the current Greek Revival meetinghouse represents a type of architecture popular with wealthy planters in this part of Georgia. Also built in the mid-eighteenth century, Bark Camp Baptist (see page 47) in Burke County (of which Jenkins County was then a part) is in the same vernacular.

The Baptist reverend Matthew Moore was pastor when Big Buckhead was organized. A Loyalist, he was the only Baptist minister in the state to side with the Tories when the Revolutionary War began in 1775. Moore fled to Savannah before returning to England shortly after, and the church became inactive during the war as a result. According to R. L. Robinson's *History of the Georgia Baptist Association*, apparently the bulk of his congregation was also Loyalist. "Although most Baptists in Georgia supported the American cause, one obscure Separate church was comprised of Tories. Existing first from 1774 to about 1776, the Big Buckhead congregation . . . was led by two notable pro-British partisans and produced George Liele, the black preacher whose concern for freedom from slavery fired his anti-American feelings."

George Liele was a slave owned by Colonel Henry Sharp, a loyalist deacon in the church. Liele was converted under the ministry of the Reverend Moore and later freed by his master prior to the Revolution in order to preach the Gospel. He helped establish the First African Baptist Church in Savannah and also became the first Baptist missionary to Jamaica, where he fled following the war.

It took a full four years after the war ended for the Big Buckhead Church to get on its feet again, many of its Tory members having fled the state. The congregation reorganized on September 11, 1787. The current meetinghouse is the fourth church to stand on or near here. The first was of logs, and the second was framed and completed in 1807 at a cost of about three hundred dollars. In 1830, the congregation, mostly local planters, funded construction of a brick church—the bricks would have been brought in at great expense—for the princely sum of about four thousand dollars. Ironically, a construction defect led to this third building being declared unsafe and ultimately dismantled. The fourth and current church was built in 1855.

Big Buckhead Church has witnessed a number of important events. Bishop Frances Asbury, first American Bishop of the Methodist Church, preached at Buckhead on January 23, 1793, and the Hephzibah Association was organized here in 1794. When the Georgia Baptist Convention met in the third, brick incarnation in 1831, it resolved to establish a school that became Mercer University (now in Macon). After the Civil War, black members left Big Buckhead to form their own nearby church, Carswell Grove (see next entry).

The Big Buckhead meetinghouse, which is opened for special events, is now privately owned.

Compared to the Greek Revival exterior, the meetinghouse interior is relatively modest and intimate. The high ceilings and sixteen-over-sixteen shuttered sash windows helped mitigate the sweltering, South Georgia heat. The crown moldings, milled window casings, corner moldings, and dentition in the altar (left foreground) reflect the quality construction and affluence of the congregation in 1855.

Two pairs of elaborately framed entry doors—
one pair for women and children, the other for men—
open into the sanctuary from behind the elevated
chancel, which is unusual. Fortunately, there was
also a rear entry door for late arrivals.

Across the road from the church, surrounded by woods, is the church's small, gated cemetery containing only eight interments ranging from 1847 to 1889. Most of the nineteenth-century planter families would have been buried in family plots on their plantations.

Built in 1855, the current church is a grand wooden structure in the Greek Revival style on a pierced brick foundation, with a full-width entry porch—an architectural tribute to the wealth of the Burke County planters who built it.

PHOTOGRAPHY BY JOHN KIRKLAND

Carswell Grove Baptist

The church seen here was the second to be built at this location by the Carswell Grove Baptist congregation. Like the first, it was destroyed by fire. Founded in 1867 in a corner of Burke County that later formed part of Jenkins County, Carswell Grove is among the oldest congregations in either county. It was started by black members who left Big Buckhead Baptist (see previous entry) after the Civil War to form their own church, first meeting under a brush arbor. The land for the church, a few hundred yards away from Big Buckhead, was donated by Judge Porter W. Carswell of Burke County, and the first structure was erected here in 1870.

Carswell Grove grew steadily after its founding to become one of the largest black congregations in Georgia. In 1919, it drew over a thousand members to worship at this backcountry church. Sadly, that year, antiblack violence, which had long been simmering, erupted on the grounds of Carswell Grove Baptist Church when two white policemen attempted to arrest a black congregant. Black bystanders objected, words were exchanged, and a huge fight broke out. Participants black and white died. The entire community was engulfed in racial strife. Riots ensued and spread. Tragically, this conflagration ultimately spread across the South and then across the nation in what became known as the Red Summer. The original church was burned in the aftermath of the riot, and the Gothic Revival structure seen here was built over the ashes in 1919. This period of racial violence is the subject of Cameron McWhirter's *Red Summer: The Summer of 1919 and the Awakening of Black America.*

As the twentieth century wore on, the once-thriving rural congregation began to dwindle until only thirty members remained in the new millennium. With insufficient resources to maintain such a large structure, the congregation built a much smaller church hard by this magnificent, but faded, Gothic church in 2008.

Carswell Grove Baptist has twice been burned to the ground, most recently on November 15, 2014. Although these photos are all that remain of the 1919 Gothic structure, may the faith that twice restored Carswell Grove Baptist comfort this church and its congregation in their newest church home.

The leaking roof and gaping windowless frames had granted unhindered access to weather and wildlife before the congregation received funding from the Georgia Department of Natural Resources (DNR) in 1995. The repairs enabled by the DNR funding sufficed to stabilize the church and temporarily protect it against the greatest natural enemies of these old treasures—water and weather—though ultimately the church succumbed to a third, manmade danger: fire.

Without pews, it's difficult to visualize the capacity of the sanctuary.
The pews original to this 1919 sanctuary had been removed to the
current church and so survived the 2014 fire.

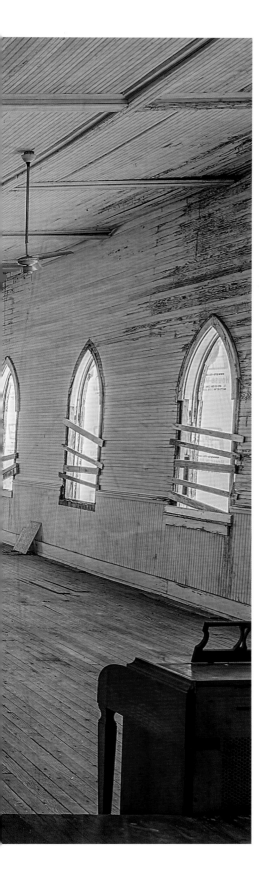

The sanctuary boasted both a small organ and this piano
(in addition to what may be a practice piano in the adjoining
room), all of which were lost in the 2014 fire.

Several generations of the Lewis family are buried in the
cemetery here. Of nearly a hundred interments in the cemetery
recorded to date, the oldest is dated 1871.

Carswell Grove Baptist has a long and proud history with an active
congregation that has worshiped here for almost 150 years.

This is what remained of the second incarnation of Carswell Grove Baptist Church after it burned to the ground on November 16, 2014. The photos attest to the fact that Carswell Grove was one of the best examples of post–Civil War rural black churches in all of Georgia. It is a sad example of how fragile these old treasures are. It will be greatly missed.

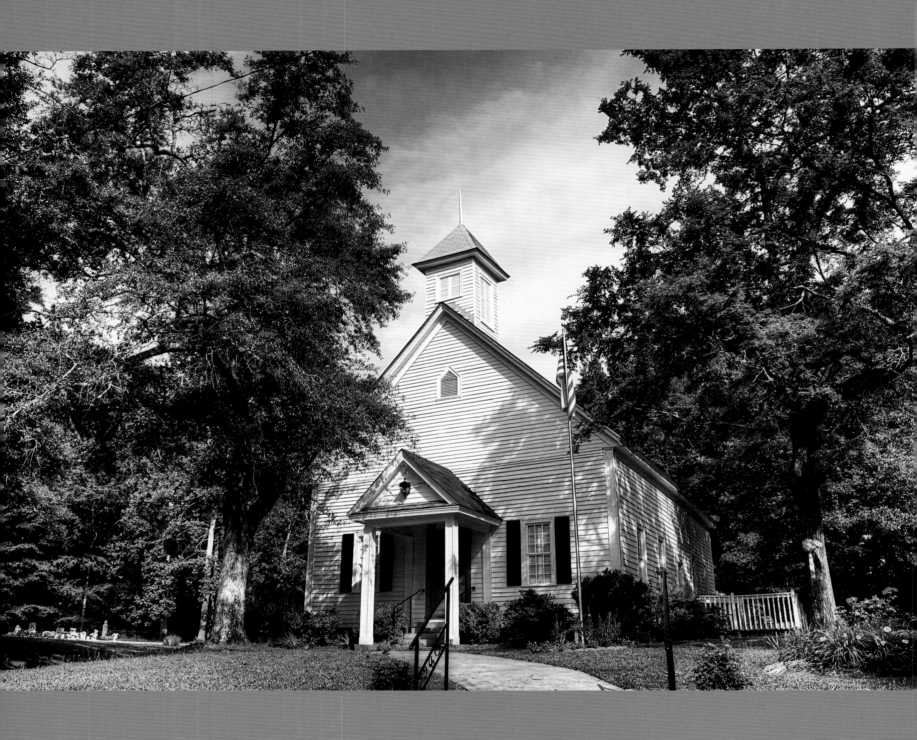

Clinton Methodist

Nestled among the trees and bordered by a beautiful cemetery, this is a perfect example
of a small, historic rural Georgia church that has been well maintained over the years.
When Clinton Methodist was founded around 1821, the town was on the edge of the
Georgia frontier. Created in 1807, Jones County lay on the western border of Georgia.
After it was chosen in 1801 as the county seat, Clinton began to grow quickly. On July
14, 1821, the Inferior Court of Jones County made out a deed to the Clinton Methodist
Church, listing five individuals as trustees. This makes Clinton Methodist one of the
oldest churches founded and built along what was then Georgia's western border in the
lower Piedmont.

In her encyclopedic *History of Jones County*, Carolyn Williams writes: "It is thought
that the present structure was erected at this period (1821). This church is a frame house
of good dimensions with substantial stone steps from the native granite. A steeple is
overhead. The windows are large and wide. Double doors form the main entrance. . . .
A large gallery which was reached by steps from the front extended over the front part
of [the interior] of the church and was for the use of Negro slaves." She goes on to
observe that in 1896 the sanctuary was completely remodeled when the slave gallery
was removed, which substantially changed the structure. By the time the county seat
had transferred in 1905, the town of Clinton was already largely defunct and Clinton
Methodist's membership began to diminish. The church was inactive for some years,
but since its reorganization in 1933 has remained active.

Adjacent to the church is the Clinton Methodist cemetery, which is filled with quarried stonework by Jacob P. Hutchings, a slave of the Hutchings family. Jake was born a slave in Virginia in 1831. He became a talented granite mason, burial site enclosure builder, and home builder. He also discovered a granite outcropping nearby that became known as Jakes Woods, where he sourced and quarried the giant blocks found throughout the Clinton Methodist Cemetery. After his emancipation, Hutchings became a prominent citizen of Clinton and served as Jones County's first black member of the Georgia State Congress in the 1870s. Jake died in 1909 and is memorialized, in granite, at the nearby Jones County Courthouse.

The church is now part of the Old Clinton Historic District and was added to the National Register of Historic Places in 1974. Clinton Methodist is still an active congregation.

The wide, double front doors at the center rear of the sanctuary
and the two wide, side aisles were part of the original, pre–Civil War
configuration. The raised chancel bridges the aisles.

This lovely old foot pump organ, although no longer in use, remains in the sanctuary as a reminder of days gone by. Despite the urbanization of Georgia, this thriving church manifests the strength of rural communities all across the state and the nation.

The entrance doors and granite steps are original. A recent church pamphlet is as inviting as the front of this lovely church: "Our church prides itself in being a very friendly, informal (blue jeans just fine) congregation who enjoys a traditional, Methodist service each Sunday at 9:45. We look forward to serving our community another two hundred or even more years."

Visible here are some of the eclectic monuments and uncommonly old gravestones at Clinton Church cemetery, which contains marked graves from the early 1800s to the present. The huge granite stones in the background here were carefully laid and lapped so as to withstand the tests of weather and time with no mortar. The person responsible for quarrying, chiseling, and laying this false crypt was Jacob "Jake" P. Hutchings.

Within this single enclosure by Jacob Hutchings are the gravestones of Peyton T. Pitts, a captain with the Twelfth Georgia Infantry (left foreground) and his widow (right foreground). Visible behind them is the cradle-style grave of a child (center middle ground) and, peeking over the grave of Captain Pitts, is a scrolled-topped, early nineteenth-century tablet.

Some of the finest wire, wrought-iron, and cast-iron grave enclosures in any rural southern graveyard are found here. Perhaps the early, monolithic granite enclosures whetted the Clintonians appetite for stylish enclosures. As the community became more sophisticated in the mid-nineteenth century, the massive, Hutchings-style enclosures began to give way to more modern and inviting metal structures. Gated iron fencing began to appear by the 1840s and remained popular among the wealthy into the early twentieth century.

Midway Congregational

This wood frame church from 1792 is reminiscent of the colonial architecture built by the richest class of English planters on the banks of the Potomac. In fact, the church was founded by wealthy planters who had migrated from the Dorchester region in South Carolina.

In 1752, the Council of Georgia made a land grant of 31,950 acres to Puritans from Dorchester in order to create a southern buffer against the Creeks and the Spanish for the emerging port of Savannah. Trustees of the Georgia colony had rescinded the law banning slavery in 1751, which allowed prosperous Carolina planters to take particular advantage of the 1752 land grant. Consequently, they flooded in to expand their operations into the Georgia Low Country. The village of Midway was founded by these new white settlers, many of them Congregationalists from South Carolina who had family roots in the Puritans of New England and, before that, England itself.

The original meetinghouse was completed in 1752 on the site of the present structure. Land was set aside for a cemetery across the road connecting Savannah with Darien and Fort Frederica.

In 1770, the populations of South Carolina and Virginia were, respectively, 124,000 and 447,000, whereas Georgia's total population, white and black, was just 23,000. This sparse Georgia population was clustered along the lower Savannah River and a narrow band along the coast south of Savannah. Almost all other land in what is now Georgia (over 30 million acres) belonged to the Creeks in the south and to the Cherokees in the north.

As the fervor for American independence was intensifying in the mid-eighteenth century, Midway's settlers were enthusiastic in their support, electing Button Gwinnett and Lyman Hall (the latter a Congregational Church member) to serve in the Continental Congress. One price the Midway patriots paid for their revolutionary zeal was the 1778 destruction of the first Midway Congregational meetinghouse. After the British had taken the town and sacked local farms, Lieutenant Colonel Jacques Marcus Prevost ordered his retreating troops to burn the church to the ground.

Fourteen years later, the current meetinghouse was completed and has been active as a church ever since. The church and the cemetery were added to the National Register of Historic Places in 1973 as part of the Midway Historic District.

From the pulpit, the view of the Midway sanctuary is of bright white paint except on the pine floors and accent wood trim (the pew seats are also unpainted). The cathedral-like architecture of the sanctuary features a tray ceiling that soars 25 to 30 feet high. Bold Doric columns support the slave gallery, which runs along three sides of the second floor and is faced by elegant, curved wood paneling. The doors at the ends of each box pew speak to the English architecture. Illuminating the entire space are six-over-six clear glass windows spaced along the first-floor walls and matched by windows above in the gallery.

The unadorned but commanding raised pulpit embodies the Puritan traditions at the heart of this church, reflecting their desire to purify the Church of England by advocating simpler, unostentatious design within their houses of worship.

The wall-mounted historical plaques flanking the pulpit are the only ornamentation in the sanctuary. The simplicity and purity the congregation sought are evident here, as is the dedication of the generations of congregants who have maintained and preserved this meetinghouse since 1792.

The huge gallery is evidence of how many slaves were needed for the success of the planters' rice, cotton, and indigo enterprises, from which the profits sprang to build this grand edifice in 1792. Seventy-odd years later, the inequity represented by this gallery would be relegated to the past.

This historic rural cemetery provides the opportunity for us to observe the evolution of materials, types, and styles of grave monuments from the mid-eighteenth into the twentieth century in Georgia. In this view are primarily mid- to late eighteenth-century tablets. The low, brick-walled boxes covered by a single ledger stone are known as false crypts.

Midway Congregational has twice been embroiled in the middle of military conflict. In 1778, the British army stormed across this ground to destroy the original meetinghouse. In 1864, Sherman's cavalry bivouacked their horses in the walled cemetery before charging into Savannah to initiate "the beginning of the end" of the Civil War. Today, Midway Congregational looks much as it did when rebuilt in 1792.

Wrightsboro Methodist

The Wrightsboro Methodist Church stands proudly on a hill where, in 1754, Edmund Grey founded what would be the very short-lived Quaker town of Brandon. In 1768, following the Treaty of Augusta, the Cherokees ceded this land to the swelling tide of European settlers. Royal Governor James Wright granted 40,000 acres of land to Joseph Mattock and Jonathan Sell, who were also Quakers. This was the southernmost point of the Quaker migration in colonial America. However, most of the Quakers soon became disillusioned with their new situation, filled with armed conflict with the British and the Indians, and returned to the North by about 1805.

Where Brandon had been sited, a thousand acres were designated for a new town and incorporated in 1799 as the city of Wrightsboro. Wrightsboro was an important settlement in early Georgia history, having two roads that were approved for construction by the Governor's Council in 1769—one from Augusta and one, known as the Quaker Road, from Savannah. The Augusta road became a stagecoach route over time, while the road to Savannah was one of the longest in the province.

According to the Wrightsboro Foundation, the locations of the current church and cemetery were established at the time of incorporation. In December 1810, the Georgia General Assembly granted the Wrightsboro town commissioners permission to use up to $500 to build "a house of worship . . . for all denominations of Christians to worship in." The current structure was the result, built in 1810–1812. The straight, clean lines of this front-gable meetinghouse with the unexpected Greek revival portico are still quite spectacular in this rural spot.

Available records pick up in 1877, when the public church was deeded to the Methodist Church South after the community agreed with the Methodists' assertion that the 2-acre property would be best served by such a transfer. By 1964, however, the Methodist congregation had disbanded after being active for over 125 years. Ownership of the church then reverted to the public as McDuffie County became caretaker. Today, the church is held by the Historic Wrightsboro Foundation.

Forbearers of several prominent Georgia families are buried alongside Wrightsboro Methodist, including those of Asa Griggs Candler—founder of the Coca-Cola Company and mayor of Atlanta from 1916 to 1919. While the original towns of Brandon and Wrightsboro have not survived, the area remains rich in interesting historic structures and stories, well worth a visit.

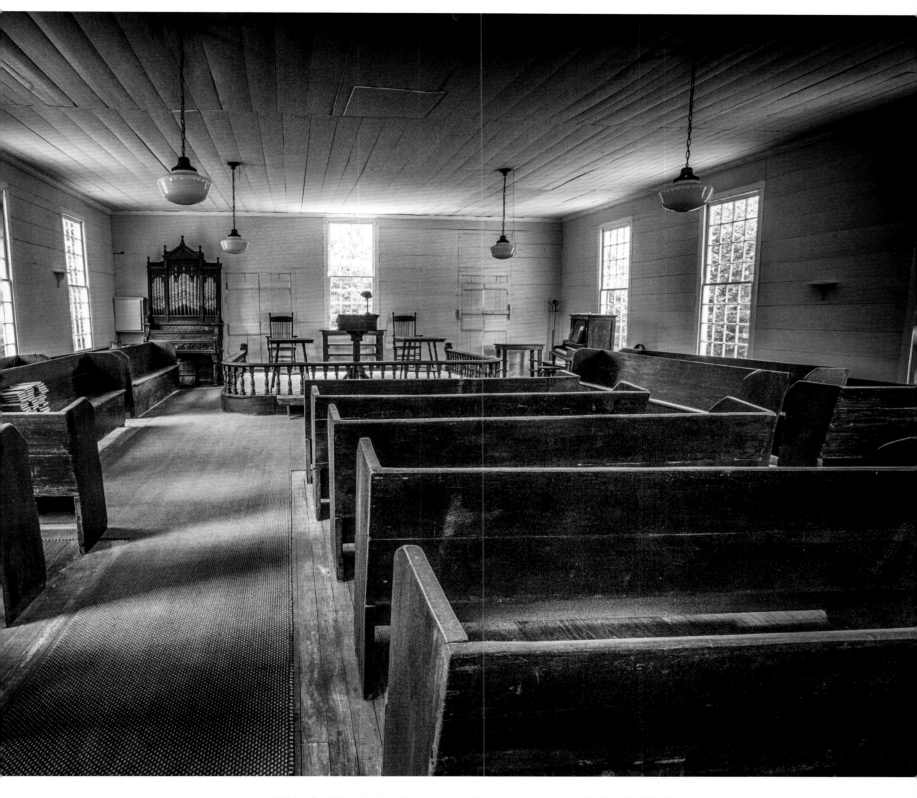

This double-aisle jewel was saved for posterity when the McDuffie County government stepped up in the mid-1960s to take possession and maintain it. Inactive as a church for the last half century, the interior has not had to keep up with the demands of a twenty-first-century congregation and gracefully reflects its early nineteenth-century lineage.

The church is outfitted with both a piano and this splendid organ. The organ is a foot-pumped, tracker style employing pipes rather than reeds. Each of the nineteen pipes exhibits artistic stenciling. The organ would have been an expensive purchase and represents the highest construction and sound quality available in its day.

OPPOSITE: Bringing light and ventilation into the sanctuary, the original sixteen-over-sixteen windows also provide a view of the cemetery studded with giant oaks. The hand-hewn pews were made around 1812 from heart pine and joined without nails.

With the double entry doors and raised chancel, most Christian denominations would have been comfortable holding services here in the nineteenth century, as indeed they did. This is a splendid interior view of a church that has survived for over two hundred years.

Veterans of the Revolutionary War and the Civil War lie in the cemetery,
including Dr. Ellington Cody Hawes. The first member of the Hawes family to be
interred here was infant Lucilius Hawes in 1854—the ninth Hawes was buried here in 1963.
The mid-nineteenth-century gravestones are indicative of a wealthy economy arising from
the rich agricultural Georgia land only recently acquired from the native inhabitants.

There are 137 documented interments in the church yard, with the oldest being an infant who died in 1800. Cemeteries this old often illustrate the evolution from unmarked graves to fieldstone or wood markers to simple tablets to more elaborate headstones that were either engraved/decorated locally or bought and shipped in. Visible in the distance are the boarded-up doors behind the chancel. The center window behind the pulpit was rather unusual.

Sapelo First African Baptist

The First African Church on Sapelo Island is a beautiful treasure of a church founded in 1866 by newly freed slaves in a section of the island known as Hanging Bull. The present church was built in Raccoon Bluff after the original structure was destroyed by a hurricane in 1898. Having been abandoned since the mid-twentieth century, it was carefully restored, beginning in 2000, through efforts of the Sapelo Island Cultural and Revitalization Society, the state of Georgia, and students from the Savannah College of Art and Design.

The result is a magnificent restoration representing a significant effort to preserve African American history in Georgia. This church exemplifies the Gullah-Geechee culture that evolved among West African immigrants to the coastal regions of South Carolina and Georgia in the seventeenth and eighteenth centuries.

Guale Indians and their predecessors inhabited Sapelo Island before the arrival of the Spanish in the seventeenth century. The Spanish established missions here to convert the native Indians while advancing the northern frontier of the Spanish Empire in the New World. One of the missions on the coast was San José de Zápala, from which the name Sapelo is derived. Created in 1793, the county is named for the McIntosh family, Scottish Highlanders who were among the earliest settlers of Georgia. The most prominent member of this illustrious family was General Lachlan McIntosh, a Revolutionary War commander of Georgia forces.

The earliest black slaves came and left with the Spanish, but English-speaking settlers reintroduced slaves in the mid-eighteenth century. The first English-owned slaves had been introduced into Sapelo from Africa in 1762 by Patrick Mackay, who bought the island and operated it as a cotton and cattle plantation. Over the next few decades the island changed hands several times, eventually passing to Thomas Spalding. In the early 1800s, Spalding, though still a young man, became the most powerful landowner in McIntosh County with the ownership of several hundred African slaves skilled in fishing, sea island cotton growing, and rice cultivation. In 1860, on the eve of the Civil War, the census indicated the Spalding family owned 252 slaves living in fifty slave houses on the island.

After Spalding's death in 1851, the 16,500-acre island changed hands a number of times. Cut off from the mainland, it was largely abandoned by its white owners during the Civil War, as were most of the Sea Islands, which then largely fell under Union control. Sapelo and the other thirteen barrier islands fell within the district that General William T. Sherman set out, in the famous Field Order No. 15 of January 16, 1865, as a place where freed blacks could establish small farms. The order was overturned later that year and the land restored to the white plantation owners, many of whom were unable to sustain their large plantations without the free labor of black slaves. The order itself produced the longer-lived phrase, "forty acres and a mule."

Tobacco magnate R. J. Reynolds Jr. became the owner of Sapelo in the 1930s and, intent on developing the island for tourism, over the years consolidated the island's African American communities to Hog Hammock, with the result that this church was abandoned by 1968 and eventually fell into an advanced state of decay.

Sapelo First African Baptist, like some other historical rural churches, is hard to find and difficult to reach.

The care with which the restoration was undertaken is apparent. The sanctuary is bright and colorful, with the gold of the pine pews echoed in the gold glass border of the windows. When the restoration of the church began in 2000, all parties involved agreed that its late nineteenth-century character needed to be retained where present and reproduced as accurately as possible. The colorful windows and the dropped lantern lighting are examples of their successful efforts. Painting the ceiling sky blue was a common custom of the time in the South.

This close-up of the chancel reveals the decorative effect
achieved with the most basic materials: by simply changing
the direction and length of plain boards, the talented Geechee
builders created a pleasing pattern. The three-arch design above
the chancel separates that area from the sanctuary nave. At the
same time, the arches and cross lift the eyes of the congregants
to the pulpit and above. The remaining open space beneath
creates an airy feeling of space in the small church.

The translucent, colored-glass windows help create a light and airy atmosphere
in the sanctuary, enhanced by white walls and yellow pews beneath the blue ceiling.
The cheerful, pastel paints used throughout reflect the Victorian era's penchant for
mixed colors in decorating homes and buildings.

The Gullah-Geechee culture is vital to understanding the history of the Low Country in South Carolina and Georgia. On this island, accessible only by boat or air, surrounded by scrub palmettos and pines within a live-oak forest, Sapelo Island First African Baptist Church remains representative of the culture's unique customs, dialects, and many artistic aspects that reflect its origin in West Africa. The exterior of the church has been restored to approximate its original 1900 appearance as well.

PHOTOGRAPHY BY WAYNE MOORE

St. Cyprian's Episcopal

In the quaint village of Darien lies St. Cyprian's Episcopal, which was consecrated in 1876 as a mission church of St. Andrew's Episcopal, also in Darien. The church honors Saint Cyprian, a North African bishop noted for his pastoral ministry and martyred in the third century. St. Cyprian's "is believed to be one of the largest tabby structures still in use in Georgia," according to the church. Used extensively in the eighteenth and early nineteenth centuries, tabby was a common Low Country building cement made of lime, sand, and oyster shells.

Located at the mouth of the north branch of the Altamaha River, Darien was settled in 1736 by European immigrants, largely through the efforts of James Oglethorpe, founder of the colony of Georgia. With America exporting large quantities of rice and cotton all over the world, Darien prospered as a seaport. However, the Civil War changed all of that. In June 1863, according to *Brown's Guide to Georgia*, "Darien was invaded, looted, and burned to the ground on June 11, 1863 by Union troops."

The story of St. Cyprian's begins after the war in the person of the Reverend James Wentworth Leigh, an English Anglican priest who had recently married Frances Kemble Butler, the daughter and heir of Pierce Mease Butler, the owner of Butler Plantation, which lay just across the river from Darien. It had been one of the largest and most successful plantations on the Georgia coast before the war, and Pierce Butler one of the largest slave owners in the nation. Frances and her husband had returned to the plantation in an attempt to restore it to profitability.

Dr. Leigh arrived on Butler Island in 1873 and soon began a project to construct a new church for blacks in Darien. He obtained plans for the new church from an English architect, and Frances Kemble Butler Leigh donated the land. Contributions were successfully solicited, and the recently freed blacks built the church mostly from local materials.

The bishop of Georgia, the Right Reverend John W. Beckwith, consecrated St. Cyprian's on April 30, 1876. Throughout most of the church's history, the local white Episcopalian church, St. Andrew's, supplied priests to St. Cyprian's. A notable exception to this policy occurred between 1892 and 1914, when the Reverend Ferdinand M. Mann, an African American priest, served St. Cyprian's. According to the church, in that twenty-two-year period, among Mann's legacies was St. Cyprian's School, "established for the education of African American children in Darien. The school served the community for many years." Still active, the two churches continue a close relationship, sharing facilities and clergy.

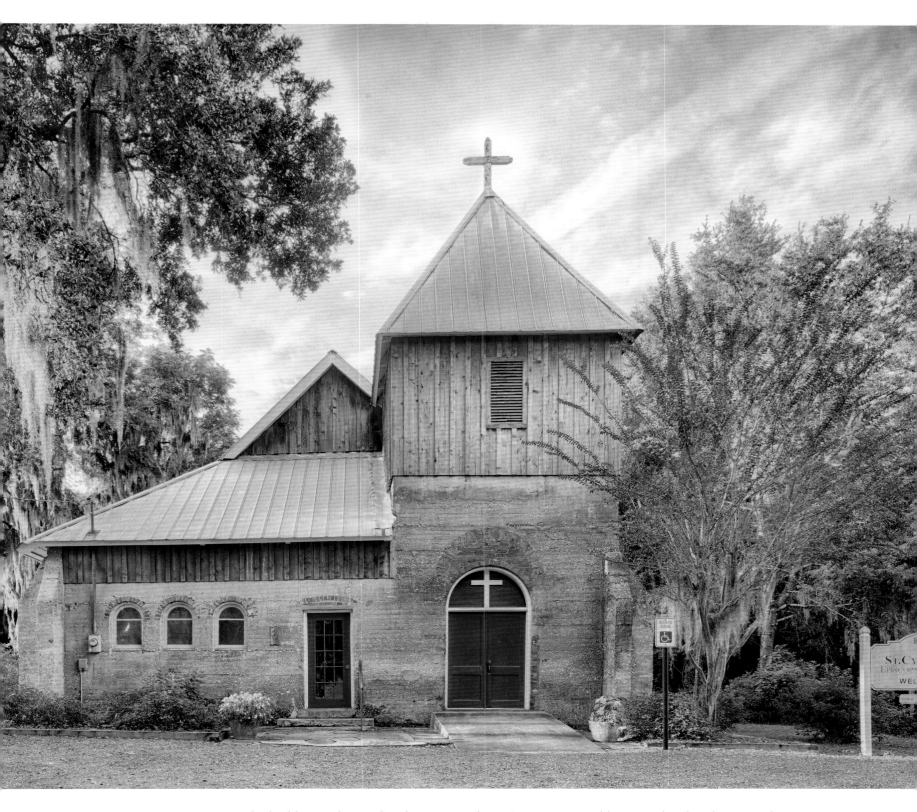

The building is designed and constructed in a Romanesque Tabby Revival style. The original 1876 structure was damaged by a hurricane in 1896 and further damaged about two years later by a tidal wave. Repair and restoration of St. Cyprian's was completed by the turn of the twentieth century. Ornamental brick around the main door and over each of the windows is visible here, a departure from the tabby construction of the foundation and the first story.

A coarse, resilient building material that has been in use since 4,000 BC, tabby is made from sand, lime (procured from the burning of oyster shells), untreated oyster shell aggregate, and water. It was commonly used in Low Country Georgia in this era, although St. Cyprian's was likely one of the last major structures built in Georgia using tabby as the primary construction material.

The sanctuary design and construction reflect the Romanesque Revival style popular in England during this period. The pews are all original and decorated with a trinity wood carving capping each end. The interior features exposed, modified scissor trusses that rise high overhead. Heavy, coffered beams and heart-pine wooden decking support the tin roof. Throughout the church are stunning, leaded glass windows. The east and west wall windows are Romanesque. Those on the north and south side walls are Gothic. All of these windows are wood framed and contain high-quality, leaded stained or painted glass. The north and south side wall windows are the most ornate and are U.S.-made Paul Wissmach and Kokomo glasses.

The chancel and altar offer a quiet study on the Trinitarian theme. The fit and finish of the wooden elements speak to the high quality of the construction.

This church is a tribute to the black community as well as to the community of Darien
as a whole, which has nurtured it since 1876. Having withstood hurricanes, a tidal wave,
the Jim Crow period, a Great Depression, and the turbulence of the civil-rights movement,
this icon of Georgia history continues to endure.

PHOTOGRAPHY BY STEVE ROBINSON

Mt. Enon Baptist

Mt. Enon Baptist Church was organized in 1856 in the Gum Pond community of Mitchell County. Originally, whites and blacks worshipped together at one service, but by 1863 the congregation had outgrown the sanctuary, so the pastor preached to the white congregation on Sunday mornings and then to over a hundred black worshippers on Sunday afternoons. After the Civil War, Mt. Enon deeded its black congregation two adjoining acres for a church building and a cemetery, and the Salem Missionary Baptist Church for Blacks was built there.

The original Mt. Enon was a one-room structure made of unpeeled logs. Because it was the only place of worship in the area, it was also used by the Methodists until 1870, when they constructed their own church. The Baptists replaced that original structure in 1889 with the larger building standing today. By 1928, membership had declined markedly but persisted, and the church enjoyed a brief revival in the 1950s, during which time some renovations and repairs were made. The revival could not be sustained, however, and in 1967 the congregation voted to close and made the decision to keep the pulpit, heaters, fans, 1950s hymnals, and piano in the building.

The cemetery behind the church has served as the burial ground for the town of Baconton since the 1860s. The church and cemetery were added to the National Register of Historic Places in 1983. Mildred Jackson Cole and the Mt. Enon Historical Committee's *From Stage Coaches to Train Whistles* was the basis for the brief historical summary above.

The sanctuary of Mt. Enon is a squarish rectangle, with a commodious vestibule and handsome, center bell tower. In this view from the pulpit we see at the rear of the sanctuary the two interior rooms and the main entry door from the vestibule. The bell is rung and reached from that area. The interior is spare and devoid of any structural decoration or unnecessary refinements. Hand hewn from heart pine and joined with wooden pegs, the pews may be those made for the original, 1856 sanctuary.

Although plain and spare, the wooden elements visible here are solid, functional, and quite pleasing to the eye. The beaded tongue-and-groove boards set horizontally on the walls are somewhat unusual and are of higher quality than one would expect in this plain sanctuary.

The ornamentation of the pulpit was achieved by skillful, diagonal presentation of the same wainscoting used to raise the small chancel and is a standout in an otherwise unadorned sanctuary. According to Cole's history, in the church's early days, mothers with small children sat in the first pew so they could lay out pallets on the floor in front of them for their children to sleep on.

The cemetery behind Mt. Enon Baptist was the site of burials not just for Baptists but for the larger Gum Pond community. The surrounding fence dates from the mid-1970s. Wooden and even fieldstone markers of many of the oldest graves would have been lost over the years, and even these robust pillars are in danger of toppling.

Still in use for a century and a half, the cemetery exhibits many styles of gravestones and memorial markers that were popular in this part of the South. In the foreground is a mid-nineteenth-century false crypt adorned with a tablet-type marker. Behind it are four slot and tablet ledger markers from the same era. The white marble headstone in the background behind the false crypt is from the twentieth century; nearby are several obelisks.

The belfry, front vestibule, and brick footings add elegance to this late nineteenth-century Baptist church. Although inactive since 1967 and seldom used today, Mt. Enon remains a reminder of how important churches were to the rural communities they served.

PHOTOGRAPHY BY SCOTT MacINNIS

Beth Salem Presbyterian

Beth Salem Presbyterian, also known as Lexington Presbyterian, is among Georgia's oldest, most prominent, and most historic rural churches. A two-time Georgia governor—George Gilmer, who served 1829–1831 and 1837–1839—and a number of early Georgia movers and shakers lie in the Beth Salem graveyard. Founded in 1785 by Pennsylvanians who moved into the area to minister to the Native Americans, Beth Salem predates the incorporation of both Oglethorpe County and the village of Lexington. In 1785, John Newton joined the group at its settlement deep in the Indian territory about three miles southwest of the present location of Lexington. On December 20, 1785, he organized the Beth-Salem Presbyterian Church (it since has lost the hyphen). From this beginning in the late eighteenth century, the county, town, and church prospered.

By 1810, at least eight meetinghouses and a dozen congregations were scattered throughout Oglethorpe County. In about 1822, the original Beth-Salem congregation reorganized itself in the town. Lexington was known for its culture, educational institutions, and commerce. However, in the 1830s, town residents fatefully voted against allowing the new Georgia Railroad to pass through the city, and Crawford, a few miles west of town, instead took that distinction. Thereafter, Lexington and Oglethorpe County's prosperity and influence began to wane, precipitating a long decline.

The congregation of Beth Salem Presbyterian built the current church in 1892, but misfortunes over the years resulted in declining membership, and in May 2015, the few remaining congregants petitioned that it be dissolved as a church. The structure had earlier been registered on the 2013 Places in Peril list of the Georgia Trust for Historic

Preservation. Since that time, and continuing until today, private citizens and the City of Lexington have joined forces to develop a preservation plan to save Beth Salem Presbyterian. Since 1976, the church has been registered as part of the Lexington Historic Site on the National Register of Historic Places.

Whereas the exterior reflects a simplified version of the Gothic Revival style, the interior features a surprising sophistication that elevates the significance of this church. The stained, coved beadboard of the ceiling bows down to meet the walls, adding decorative elegance while also visually raising the ceiling. The large arch on the end wall mimics the arched windows and draws the eye into the apse, which is illuminated by Gothic windows on either side.

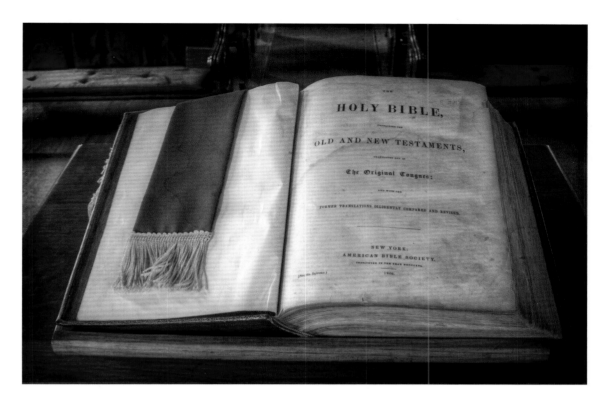

Most of the nineteenth-century furniture, fixtures, pews,
Communion silver, Bibles, and texts remain in the sanctuary.
This nineteenth-century Bible is ready at the pulpit.

OPPOSITE: In the early twentieth century, this window near the front of
the sanctuary replaced the simple geometric style of the original window.
It honors Francis Upson, 1814–1886, the son of Stephen Upson. Upson
County is named for Stephen.

Just inside this gated enclosure in the cemetery are two false crypts,
a favored antebellum style. The heavy, elaborate cast-iron fencing
surrounding some of the family plots probably predates the Civil War.
Among the family enclosures in this cemetery are the Simses, Uptons,
Remberts, Coxes, and McKinleys—all prominent families.

This view is from the west side of the church into several of the family plots. Some of the cast-iron fencing is as heavy and elaborate as one will find in any southern rural graveyard, likely predating the Civil War. The monument in right background with the urn on top is another variant of the pedestal tomb, pedestal tomb urn.

Philomath Presbyterian

This church has changed names and moved at least three times since 1788, when it was organized as Liberty Presbyterian by the Reverend Daniel Thatcher. The name Liberty was apparently chosen because other Christian denominations also held services in the log building located near War Hill.

The second church, named Salem, was built 7 miles away from the log house, and the third was located near present-day Washington. By 1848, the Presbyterians occupied their fourth church home in the town of Woodstock, soon renamed Philomath, and the church name was changed to reflect its new location. The current building replaced the 1848 structure about 1900. This frame church, the congregation's fifth, is especially notable for its Gothic Revival stained-glass windows and the corner bell tower that proudly stands as the dominant architectural feature. Regular services ceased here in the 1960s.

Behind the current church, the municipal cemetery has been in use since the early 1850s. Both are part of the Philomath Historic District, added to the National Register of Historic Places in 1979. Beginning in the early 2000s, the church was carefully restored by the community, which included extensive repairs to the foundation.

The well-crafted cove ceiling and heart-pine floors are beautiful as well as functional. The Gothic Revival windows, doors, and pews are among the features attended to in the restoration. Of note are the rectangular window frames that surround the pointed, Gothic windows. This clever design allows the installation of sashed windows whose lower, square section can be raised open. This allowed better circulation of air than the usual Gothic windows that swung open (and stuck out).

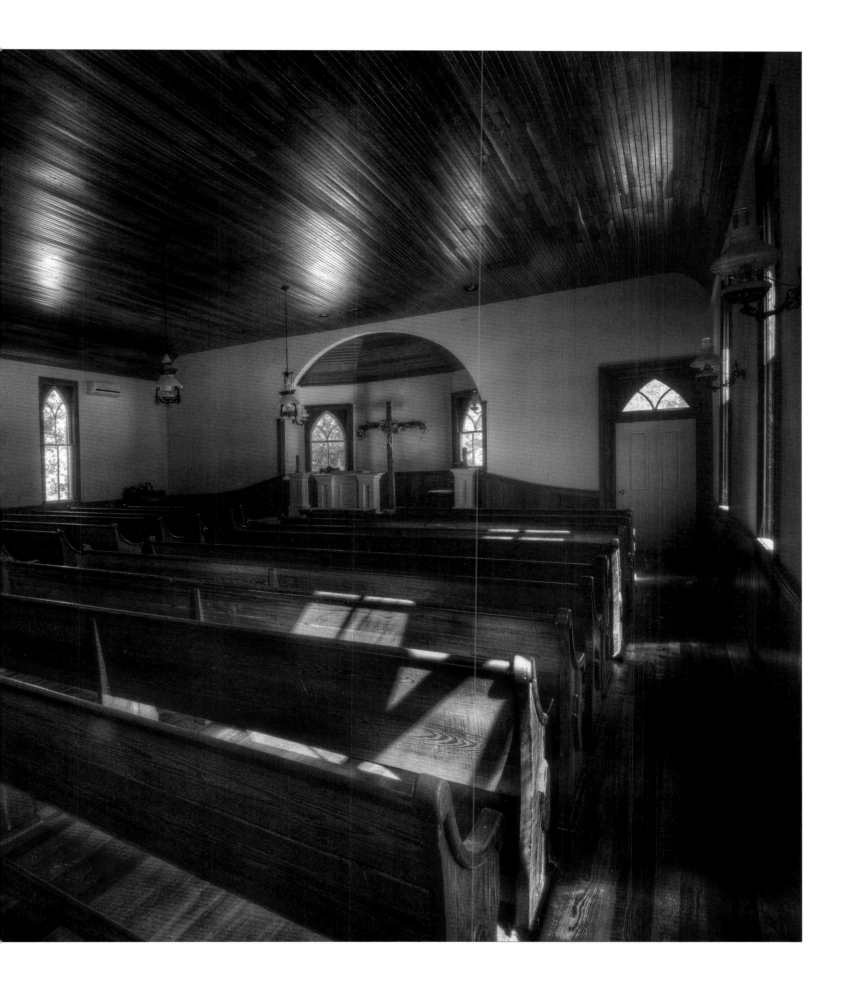

The quality of materials is particularly evident in the pews as well as the Gothic arched windows mentioned earlier. As you can see, the pews were top of the line for the era and incorporate graceful scrolled armrests as well as applied pew-end medallions.

OPPOSITE: The apse is a cameo of the sophistication of the original architectural design and the exceptional quality of the carpentry visible throughout the church. The ceiling in the apse traces the complexity of the exterior segmented roof. The eye is also drawn to the pulpit and candle pillar, which are painted white and adorned with stacked molding.

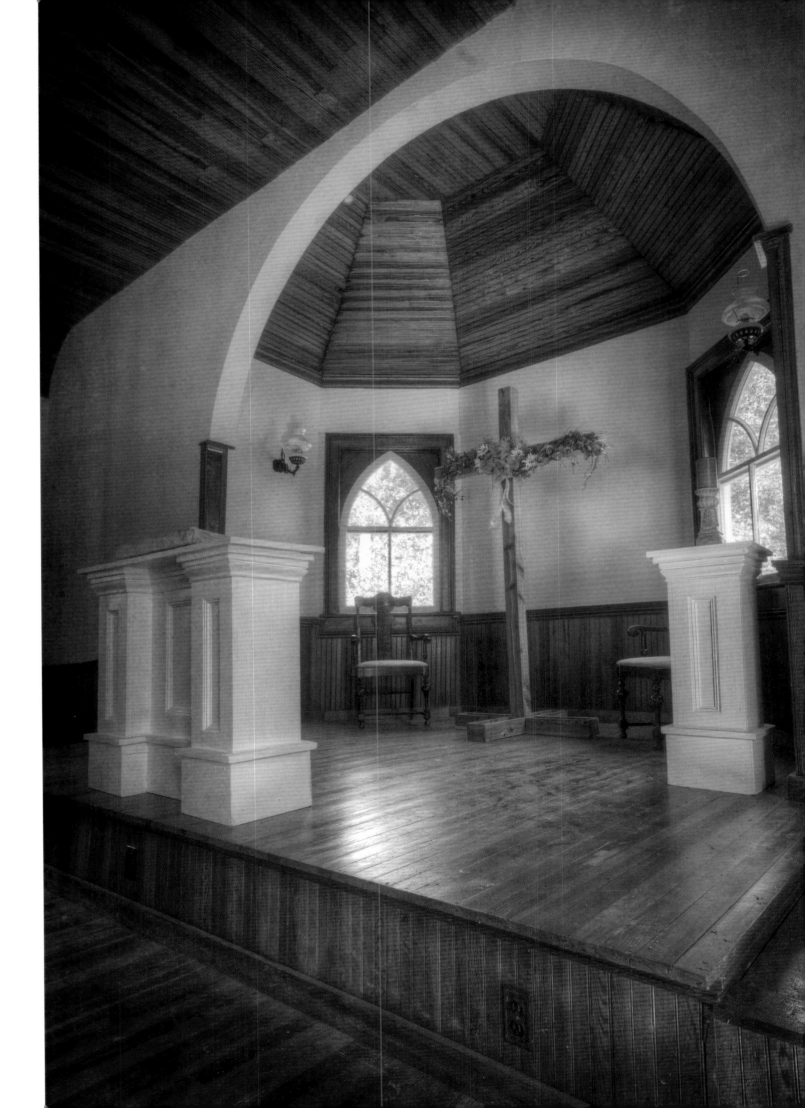

The door at the rear of the sanctuary leads to a small vestibule,
from which the bell tower can also be accessed.

The town cemetery behind the church dates to the 1850s. Of the seventy-five documented interments here, the oldest is that of William Daniel, who died in 1858. The largest family group is that of the Nash family, whose graves span the years from 1905 to 2010.

PHOTOGRAPHY BY SCOTT MacINNIS

Van Wert Methodist

The town of Van Wert was named for Isaac Van Wert, who assisted in the capture of Benedict Arnold's coconspirator, British army major John André. The town of Van Wert was settled by whites through the usual process of acquiring Cherokee land and doling it out in small increments through the lottery system. This part of the state lay in Paulding County until 1851, when Polk County was formed.

It is likely the first church in the area was the Van Wert Church of Christ Baptist, which established itself in 1840 in a nearby log structure. When the local Methodists organized in 1846, they built the current church, which they then shared with the Baptists until about 1850. The discovery of local slate in 1849 boosted the Van Wert economy and brought in Welsh miners, many of whom joined the Methodist congregation.

Van Wert was where Samuel Porter Jones began his Methodist ministry career in 1872. Having been called to the ministry after his father's death earlier that year, Jones renounced alcohol, which had nearly ruined his life, and started preaching in the Van Wert circuit, five churches spread over four counties. He went on to preach around the country to huge crowds and within twenty years was among the most famous preachers in the United States.

From its beginnings until the latter half of the twentieth century, this Van Wert meetinghouse was a church home to or seeded seven local congregations that remain active, including Church of God and Presbyterian in addition to Baptist and Methodist. Church minutes from when this was a Baptist congregation remind us that early churches were the keepers of the morals of the community and addressed these matters through an established process, as in the example that follows.

February 15, 1845: "Brethren Hogue and Spratling offered acknowledgments for buying lottery tickets, which was received. Also Brother Roach came forward and offered acknowledgment for getting mad and using bad language and buying a lottery ticket, which was received. Also Brother Thomas came forward and offered acknowledgment for getting drunk, which was received."

Replacing the words "acknowledgment" with "admission of guilt" and "received" with "pardoned" provides the law-and-order context for the role rural churches played in the period, regardless of denomination.

Van Wert Methodist is no longer an active church. For the past decade, the Euharlee Valley Historic Society has undertaken the daunting task of gathering local resources and volunteers to restore and preserve the structure for use by the community.

Through the large windows, light pours into the sanctuary. Those attending special events, reunions, or occasional services can today enjoy modern electricity and plumbing in the mid-nineteenth-century building. The door to the left of the modest chancel provides a glimpse of the sacristy and annex, into which the small apse is tucked.

Locally available building materials were used in the construction of the church in 1846. These clapboards and window frames are original, although modern windows were installed in the last quarter of the twentieth century.

OPPOSITE: Many of the replacement windows in this church are dedicated to the memory of former members, some of whom are buried in the historic cemetery on the rolling hills behind the church.

Sarah Strickland's resting place in the Van Wert cemetery is surrounded by a dry wall of local slate. The nearby slate mines brought work and relative prosperity to the small settlement. Strickland, born in 1779, lived to the age of 102 and was placed in this graveyard in 1881—an extraordinary longevity in the Georgia backcountry.

Here lies Albert Anderson, Ballentine's Rangers, Second Mississippi Cavalry. Young Albert enlisted very late in the war, in June 1864, when the South was desperately recruiting older men and boys in defense of the homeland. He was killed on October 10, 1864, in his first skirmish right here in Van Wert, as Sherman and John Bell Hood were regrouping after the Battle of Atlanta. He was sixteen years old. He is buried here in the Van Wert churchyard near where he fell.

The architecture and design of the Van Wert meetinghouse distinguish it from other rectangular, center-gable churches. The center steeple, set back from the facade and incorporated into the roof trussing for strength, is unusual. Today the structure remains relatively faithful to the original.

This photograph from the 1930s breathes life into the statement that these
old churches were the justice, social, religious, and moral center about which
the community orbited. Rich and poor, young and old, male and female—
their lives revolved around the churches.

PHOTOGRAPHY BY STEVE ROBINSON

Benevolence Baptist

Benevolence Baptist came into being during the period in Baptist history in which the biblical basis for mission work became a divisive issue. Benevolence Baptist developed from two earlier local churches, changing names as they switched affiliation to new or existing Baptist associations.

In 1840, the congregation of nearby Walnut Grove Baptist split nearly evenly over whether to remain in the Bethel Association, which had just adopted a pro-missionary position. As noted in Alexander Lee Miller's *History of Bethel Association Including Centennial Meeting*, "the missionary half [of the Walnut Grove congregation], rather than give up their conscientious conviction with reference to the duty of benevolence, came together with a few from other churches and were constituted into a church May 16th, 1840, by James Mathews and Isaac Osteen. As a matter of zeal and triumph of principle they named their newly organized church Benevolence," which was the name used to describe mission and education ministries in the era. The name alone would have identified the church as a "Missionary" Baptist church.

According to the Georgia Historical Commission marker outside the church, the benevolence of local resident Thomas Coram in donating 5 acres of land for this new church may instead be the source of the name, both for the church and the community that sprang up here. The first structure was dedicated in May 1842.

With Mathews called as the first pastor, the membership of Benevolence Church grew rapidly from the original fourteen members throughout the rest of the nineteenth century. As quoted by Miller, Pastor William Norton observed in 1879 that "though the times are changed, yet they purpose to never be unmindful of the struggles of the past and the principles then so dear."

The present sanctuary, Benevolence's second, was built around 1900 in the Carpenter Gothic style then popular. This church is more flamboyant than most constructed at this time and reflects the confidence and wealth of its prosperous congregation at the turn of the twentieth century. Its Gothic design incorporates an articulated side steeple—very fashionable at that time. The metal roof of the steeple has tapered eves and four miniature versions of the main steeple. This ornamentation was a typical way to terminate a pitched roof and provide weather protection. The large finial at the apex also provides decoration as well as roof protection. Benevolence would have been an expensive church to design and was certainly one of the most grand in Randolph County at that time.

The ceiling in the sanctuary is one of the significant design and decorative elements of Benevolence. The trussed-rafter roof design incorporates two angled sections joined by a central, level panel. All the weight is borne by the rafters, but no beams need to be exposed. This allowed the use of flat-laid, stained heart-pine tongue-and-groove ceiling boards, which have been arranged in patterns.

An unusual feature is that the wainscoting along the wall repeats the angled pattern of the center ceiling boards. These factory-produced pews are adorned with scrolled arm rests and handsome, decorative pew-end wooden plaques.

From the raised chancel, one feels the intimacy of this compact sanctuary. The huge Gothic stained-glass windows bathe the space in soft light. These windows can be unlocked and swung out on side-mounted pin swivels. This is a particularly valuable feature on hot summer Sundays. The door on the right leads directly outside, whereas the door on the left leads into a small vestibule in the steeple before leading outside.

The pillar in the foreground marks the grave of Capt. James T. Harden, Company F, Eighteenth Georgia Infantry, who survived his service during the Civil War. Just behind the gravestone is a wonderful example of nineteenth-century cast-iron fencing. The cemetery at Benevolence also contains a number of high-quality cast-iron grave enclosures, reflecting the wealth of the congregation in the nineteenth century.

The careful plantings, lattice crawl-space enclosure, and grounds are further proof that Benevolence is carefully maintained and has been throughout the years. That excellent stewardship is evident today. And the expense and love invested by its builders reflect the prosperity of the once-thriving agrarian village in the Georgia backwoods. Much has changed in Randolph County since its heyday, but Benevolence still stands, serves its congregation, and speaks reverently to us today.

PHOTOGRAPHY BY STEVE ROBINSON

Antioch Primitive Baptist

Founded in 1832 in Pleasant Valley, Antioch Primitive Baptist Church did not move to this small farm community in western Stewart County until 1851. At that time the area was known as Hannahatchee, after a local creek, although in 1887 the small community was renamed Louvale. The original log church was replaced in the mid-1880s with this structure, the first of three late nineteenth-century church buildings to be built in what became known as Louvale Church Row.

This cluster of churches, now on the National Register of Historic Places, emerged through the efforts of Dr. William H. Tatum, who in the late 1880s envisioned Louvale as a future terminus railroad town on the Americus, Preston and Lumpkin Railroad line. To help build up what he hoped would be the social nucleus of the new town of Louvale, Tatum acquired land alongside the Antioch church and its schoolhouse. By 1892, however, it was clear that the railroad line would bypass Louvale, ultimately resulting in the failure of the little village to grow beyond a rural Georgia farming community. Tatum later donated the land so that Methodist and Baptist congregations could build their own houses of worship, thus Louvale Church Row.

Despite its Primitive Baptist legacy, the church is elegant. The center steeple design, with the narrow roof overhang spanning the front of the church, is unusual, particularly in nineteenth-century backwoods Georgia. Tall windows along three sides and in the shallow apse balance the architectural design while allowing ample light and ventilation into the sanctuary.

Having ceased services in the 1950s, Antioch Primitive Baptist underwent repair and restoration in the early 1980s and again became an active church.

A center aisle as wide as the chancel adds to the dramatic impact of the sanctuary of Antioch Primitive Baptist Church. Light pours in through the four-over-four windows, as if to bring the countryside inside. The squarish, primitive pews and the wainscoting are painted pastel blue, a marked contrast to the unpainted pulpit and the white upper walls.

Notable features here are the detailed woodworking of the pulpit, the hand-carved molding around the apse arch, and the decorative carving on the two wooden chairs behind the pulpit. On the back wall of the apse, the diagonal beadboard seems to point directly to the dark wooden cross. The narrow windows on either side of the apse open to allow good cross ventilation.

The small vestibule projecting from the main entrance
also projects into the structure, resulting in this unusual
configuration at the rear of the sanctuary.

One cannot overestimate the importance of music within the rural church community. Most churches would have either a piano or a pump organ, and some had both. This pump organ is a fine example of U.S. craftsmanship by the Hinners Organ Company out of Pekin, Illinois.

PHOTOGRAPHY BY STEVE ROBINSON

Plains Baptist

A village of fewer than seven hundred people in the farming region of Southwest Georgia is home to Plains Baptist Church. Europeans began to settle here in the 1820s after federal treaties with the Native Americans forced them farther west. The arrival of railroad access in the 1880s acted as a magnet for development, resulting in the consolidation of the original settlements of Lebanon, the Plains of Dura, and Magnolia Springs into the new community of Plains. The town is best known as the hometown of U.S. president and Nobel Peace Prize winner Jimmy Carter and his wife, Rosalynn.

The congregation of Lebanon Baptist—today Plains Baptist Church—has worshipped in four churches. Twenty people organized the church on December 1, 1848, calling the Reverend Jesse Stallings as pastor. In 1849 they were able to build their first church in the original settlement of Lebanon, near the center of the present-day Lebanon Cemetery. Services were held monthly for both whites and slaves as the congregation grew. According to a church document, after the Civil War "our colored brethren and sisters requested letters of dismissal." Those letters were granted on March 19, 1870, and the freed slaves formed their own congregation, the New Lebanon Baptist Church. The white congregation subsequently built a new, larger sanctuary on the original site, dedicating it in December 1870.

After the Civil War, the church, as well as the nearby town of Plains, continued to prosper. In the late 1880s, the decision was made to move to a new, in-town sanctuary, again larger than its predecessors. This third home for Lebanon Baptist Church was on South Bond Street in Plains. However, the congregation again outgrew the space, and less than twenty years later, in 1906, the current structure was erected. In 1909 the name was changed to Plains Baptist Church. The church has remained active since its founding in 1848.

Lebanon Cemetery, 1½ miles to the west, continues to accept remains and has over a thousand recorded interments.

Each transept features a tall, double stained-glass window with a single window on either side. Near the top of each gable is a circular window, just visible here high in the north transept. These windows can be opened to allow for good circulation in the warm months, a necessity in Plains's humid climate. Notice the original pews are bowed slightly toward the pulpit.

High-quality carpentry and thoughtful furnishings merge to create this elegant vignette. The undulating chancel softens the straight lines of the trim, gable roof, and wainscoting of the apse, thereby also suggesting the curved tops of the Gothic windows, as do the seatbacks of the chairs in the apse and the carving in the pulpit.

This is a view toward the rear of the church showing the entrance wall's doors, handsome transoms, and the south transept windows. The illumination from the rear coupled with that from both sides of the sanctuary introduces even more light into the space. Note that the transoms over each of the doors and the circular windows high in the gables are filled with stained glass. The white-painted panels in the high, vaulted ceiling seem to soar above the elegant, dark-stained pews.

Local Baptists built their first sanctuary in 1849 in the small community of Lebanon. The center of historic Lebanon Cemetery is the approximate location of that original church. This false-crypt style ("false" because the body is buried in the ground below the crypt) visible in the foreground began to be popular in the late eighteenth century.

The flat landscape on which Lebanon Cemetery lies suggests
nineteenth-century familiarity with the biblical book of Daniel,
which mentions "the plain of Dura, in the province of Babylon."
The oldest legible grave is from 1843 (John Rhymes Davenport,
1839–1843), suggesting that the burial ground may predate the
first church at this location.

PHOTOGRAPHY BY STEVE ROBINSON

St. Mark's Lutheran

German immigrants moving into Georgia from South Carolina organized St. Mark's Lutheran in the late 1860s and built their church in 1870 in the now defunct community of Botsford, about five miles west of Plains. Now privately owned, the church building was moved to a lot nearby and restored, and we are fortunate to have photographs of the church both before and after restoration. The cemetery at the original location remains undisturbed.

Most of Georgia's early pioneers were English and Scots-Irish and were predominantly Baptist and Methodist, with Presbyterians running a distant third. Therefore, Lutheran churches are rare in rural Georgia. However, the early settlers of Botsford were immigrants of German descent from what are now Newberry and Lexington Counties in South Carolina. Some descendants of these early German Lutherans are still in the area.

Church records are scarce, and it is unknown when the church became inactive. The current owners occasionally open the church to the public and for special events.

A private party shouldered the responsibility for saving St. Mark's,
moving it from this original location and restoring it with care.

Partly because the structure did not suffer from leaks, rot, or foundation problems,
the attractive, authentic style of this 1870 church was still intact before the restoration.

As part of the restoration, the wall covering and
ceiling tiles were removed, revealing these original
wide pine boards on the ceiling and walls. The original
heart-pine floors and other interior pine features have
been refinished. The original pews have been replaced
with a more decorative style and spaced wider apart
for modern comfort.

The original windows are tall but extend almost to the floor. This arrangement allows those seated in the pews to gaze out at the Georgia rural countryside in the church's new location.

The church and the cemetery are about the same age, and before the church
was moved and restored, the cemetery lay hard by the apse. The first identifiable
interments were in 1871, three of them for infants who were all under three
months of age at their deaths. Infant mortality was quite high in the backcountry
into the twentieth century. The most recent interment here was in 1968.

Antioch Baptist

As you drive down old Georgia 22 between Crawfordville and Powelton, it is impossible to miss the beautiful sanctuary that is Antioch Baptist Church. Records for the church are scarce, but we think the Antioch Baptist Church was constructed in 1899. According to a church document provided by one of the members, "After the Civil War, the sons and daughters of ex-slaves in south Taliaferro County and North Hancock County had a vision of expanding their freedom and shaping their own lives as they saw fit. So, a group of courageous pioneers from the Powelton New Hope Baptist Church, led by Deacon Willie Peak, Deacon Abe Frazier and Deacon Philic Jones, came together and founded the Antioch Baptist Church in Taliaferro County, outside of Crawfordville, on November of 1886. The deacon board purchased two acres of land from the Veazey estate and two acres were deeded to them for a cemetery."

Its design is quite different from many other local Baptist churches from the same period, which were, for the most part, a basic box construction that may or may not have had a steeple. It doesn't look entirely at home in such a rural part of Georgia. Flanking the main gabled structure are two substantial but squat towers in the Gothic Revival style popular from the 1820s through the early twentieth century.

The twin towers flanking the covered porch, along with the Gothic arched windows are uncommon design elements in rural Baptist churches. According to a former member, "Antioch fell victim to a fire in 1921 but her spirit stood strong

and the building was reconstructed in 1923. Upon the death of Deacon
George Turner in February of 1992, the church ceased to meet on
a regular basis." The building now suffers from neglect and lack of
maintenance, resulting in serious structural issues.

This beautiful sanctuary was built by the children of freed slaves
seeking a better life. It deserves a better fate than slow decay.

Wainscoting provides a durable lower wall, though it is infrequently seen without a dado rail on top to protect the edges. The triangular transoms may be unique to Antioch. By cutting a rectangular window pane on the diagonal the clever and frugal builders used standard stock to evoke a Gothic Revival lancet window from an ordinary, six-over-six double-hung window.

The sturdy, boxy pews complement the quiet dignity and simplicity of the space, which has not been used regularly as a church since 1992. Although difficult to see here, the door to the right of the chancel leads directly outside. The windows behind the pulpit are in the apse, which may have been added sometime after construction of the sanctuary.

Antioch Baptist would benefit from attention before the structure
deteriorates further. Weather is beginning to penetrate the sanctuary,
and structural problems are emerging underneath.

The oldest documented grave in the cemetery is that of the
Reverend William Darden, who was buried in 1898. There are
seventy-one documented interments, but like many of the
older graveyards, this cemetery also contains unmarked graves.
A cemetery census of Taliaferro County conducted in 1977 revealed
there were thirty-two documented graves with headstones and
seventy-three unmarked graves that had been identified by
Deacon George Turner.

PHOTOGRAPHY BY SCOTT FARRAR

Locust Grove Catholic

Founded in the community of Locust Grove in 1790 and then moved to the farm town of Sharon in 1877, the Church of the Purification of the Blessed Virgin Mary is the oldest Catholic church in the state. According to William Harden's *History of Savannah and South Georgia*, in 1790 several Catholic families of English descent made their way from Maryland to "that part of Warren county which later became part of Taliaferro county, the cradle of Catholicity in Georgia." Thus the first Roman Catholic church in the state was established on the Georgia frontier in 1790.

The first recorded priest here was Father John LeMoin, also from Maryland. Within a few years, the English were joined by French and Irish Catholics who had been driven from their distant homes by war, famine, or other traumatic events. The first structure, probably a log cabin, was built in 1801, and a wood-frame church was constructed on the same site in 1821. In 1818, the first Roman Catholic school in the state, Locust Grove Academy, was established.

The community of Locust Grove developed into something of a Catholic epicenter in Georgia. In 1877 the parish and the church building itself were moved a half mile to Sharon, a prosperous railroad community that had sprung up after the rail line was built in the 1850s. The parish was renamed the Church of the Purification of the Blessed Virgin Mary. In Sharon the congregation continued to prosper, outgrowing the 1821 structure within a few years, and in 1883 the present clapboard church was built. A year later, Locust Grove Academy relocated to a new building alongside the church and was renamed Sacred Heart School for Boys. The Locust Grove Cemetery remains at the original location of the church, about a half mile away.

In 2014, the Georgia Trust for Historic Preservation added the church to its 2014 list of Places in Peril. The Friends of Purification Church is a coalition engaged in efforts to save this historic structure, which no longer has an active congregation and is now opened for worship only a few times a year.

In contrast to the building's rather boxy architecture, which is reminiscent of Protestant churches, the ornamentation and furnishings in this church reflect its eighteenth-century Roman Catholic origins. Substantial side altars flank the chancel. The center aisle is unusually wide given the length of the pews.

A freestanding confessional is tucked beneath the balcony at the rear of the nave. Just visible on both columns flanking the entrance doors are fonts for holy water.

The Stations of the Cross and other iconic images hang between the towering, twelve-over-twelve windows. Note the low wainscoting on the back wall. The windows at the rear of the nave illuminate a balcony supported by narrow columns capped by arched fretwork. Since this balcony was built in 1883, it was not a slave gallery. However, many pre–Civil War parishioners were substantial slaveholders, and the church minutes show a multitude of births, baptisms, and even weddings for the black members of the congregation. This was a highly unusual situation in antebellum rural Georgia.

Opposite the confessional
is this baptismal font.
The heart-pine floors,
wood wainscoting below
the plastered walls, soaring
window frames, and ornately
carved pews suggest the
talent and artistry of
the builders.

Despite the fact that only a few events are held here each year, the church appears
to have been readied for Mass to be said. The altar rail spanning the entire front of the
church and separating the congregation from the formal sanctuary has largely disappeared
from active Roman Catholic churches since Vatican II.

At the original Locust Grove
cemetery, the oldest gravestone
is dated 1826. Buried here are
many of the congregation's
original Marylanders and Irish
families—some of the oldest
Roman Catholic graves in
the state. Of the sixty-eight
documented interments in
the cemetery, those with Irish
surnames are heavily represented.
Latin inscriptions reflect the
Catholic and Gaelic origins of
the deceased.

PHOTOGRAPHY BY GAIL DES JARDIN

Cove Methodist

Cove Methodist is a beautiful and peaceful sanctuary located a few miles from the Chickamauga battlefield. In September 1863, the Battle of Chickamauga, the first major battle fought in Georgia, produced the second-highest number of casualties in the war, exceeded only by the Battle of Gettysburg. The *History of Cove United Methodist Church* records the church's beginnings this way: "In the period just after the Civil War, when times were hard and bitter, the founders of this church wanted to create a just and fitting place in which to worship God in spirit and truth. In a time when their world was struggling to rebuild itself, and the stirring events of war were still fresh in the minds of some, this history began."

The place they chose to do this was just a few miles from the 1863 battlefield. So, in March 1872, Cove Methodist Episcopal Church was established in the McLemore's Cove area, with 2 acres of land deeded to the trustees, half the land to be used for a church and the other half for a community cemetery. A frame church was erected at the foot of Lookout Mountain shortly thereafter, and in 1894 the church tore down that structure and replaced it with the current one.

According to the 1975 church history, local stone was used for the foundation and entry steps. As is the case with many rural churches, the name of Cove Methodist's designer has not survived, though that person seems to have been "schooled in the Northern part of the country, for the structure is of New England Colonial frame architecture, with its simple principles of line and proportions." The flared sides of the belfry, cedar shingling, and steep peaks over the entrance doors in particular speak to that heritage.

Although Cove United Methodist ceased being an active church in 1983, its current owner makes it available for special events and weddings.

The impact of the pristine condition of the sanctuary is enhanced by the cathedral-like ceiling, which follows the roof line before leveling off in the center of the church. This building technique is common throughout rural churches in Georgia constructed during the nineteenth century, whether they be grand or humble, large or small. This trussed-rafter design allows high ceilings without visible support columns within the sanctuary.

The semicircular chancel is unusual because it has two tiers. In this view, the dark cross against the white-plastered wall has a calming effect and announces that this quiet sanctuary is a holy place.

Although we have seen narrow-board ceilings before, here the boards glow in the light pouring through the generous windows. At the rear of the nave, a subtle double-cross feature is created by the addition of transoms above the triple window. The plastered walls and the quantity of light entering the building undermine one's sense of the church's modest dimensions. Note that the front center pew is slightly set back, as it would have been in the days when the church was heated by a large, potbellied stove just in front of the altar rail.

The fine carpentry that went
into the double-hung windows and
the wainscoting is apparent here, as
is the proximity of the cemetery.
The chair rail above the wainscoting
is unusually ornate, hinting at
the wealth that had accrued in
this parish by 1894, the date of
construction.

Eliza Glenn Cumpton and her first husband, John Glenn, who are buried
here, had a farm just up the road located within the Chickamauga battlefield.
When John was killed in the service of the Confederacy in 1862, Eliza became
the Widow Glenn. During the Battle of Chickamauga in 1863, the Union
Army's major general William Rosecrans used the Glenn farmhouse as his field
headquarters, and it was subsequently destroyed in the action. Thus the Glenn
farm location lives in Chickamauga history as the Widow Glenn's Hill.

OPPOSITE: Cove Methodist represents a late nineteenth-century trend
in Georgia toward more sophisticated church architecture featuring a
center or corner and occasionally a triple-steeple design, sometimes even
turret-like towers. This reflected the growing refinement and wealth of
Georgians after Reconstruction, even those living in rural areas.

Ezekiel New Congregational Methodist

Near this U.S. Route 1 crossroads outside of Waltertown, the sad remains of
one of the most striking churches in the Georgia backcounty are barely standing.
The church was built in 1899 by Manning Thigpen, a Congregational preacher,
and named for his twelve-year-old son Ezekiel, who died in 1889. The church
served the community that became known as Pebble Hill and once had a
one-room schoolhouse located beside it.

Ezekiel has a sister church, also in Ware County (see next entry).
The most meaningful difference between these two examples of Carpenter
Gothic architecture is that Old Ruskin has been well cared for throughout its
life, whereas Ezekiel fell into disuse in the last quarter of the twentieth century.
This is unfortunate because some restoration efforts had been made in the late
1960s. However, the eventual disappearance of the congregation resulted in the
abandonment of the church, leading to the condition visible now.

For much of this information on Ezekiel, we are indebted to Robert Latimer
Hurst's "Much History in Abandoned Ezekiel Church."

Once the roof failed, the church was susceptible to whatever further
damage the weather could deliver. Scavengers, squatters, and other intruders
accelerated the disintegration of the structure. The only partially intact
window remaining, visible at far left, suggests that the original windows
were clear six-over-six panes.

The painstaking design and ornamentation of the exterior are
visible here and in the next photograph, as is the inexorable
damage to the structure. The Carpenter Gothic style in which
the church was built dictated its steep pitched roofs, gingerbread
ornamentation, fancy scrollwork, and decorative shingle patterns.

Even in this advanced state of decay, the detailed scrollwork
on the bargeboards and elaborate shingling are unmistakably
characteristic of Carpenter Gothic architecture.

OPPOSITE: The collapse of this fine example of Carpenter Gothic
architecture will be an unfortunate loss to rural Georgian culture and
history. With the right vision and an influx of ready hands (and open
purses), a complete restoration is not out of the question—yet.

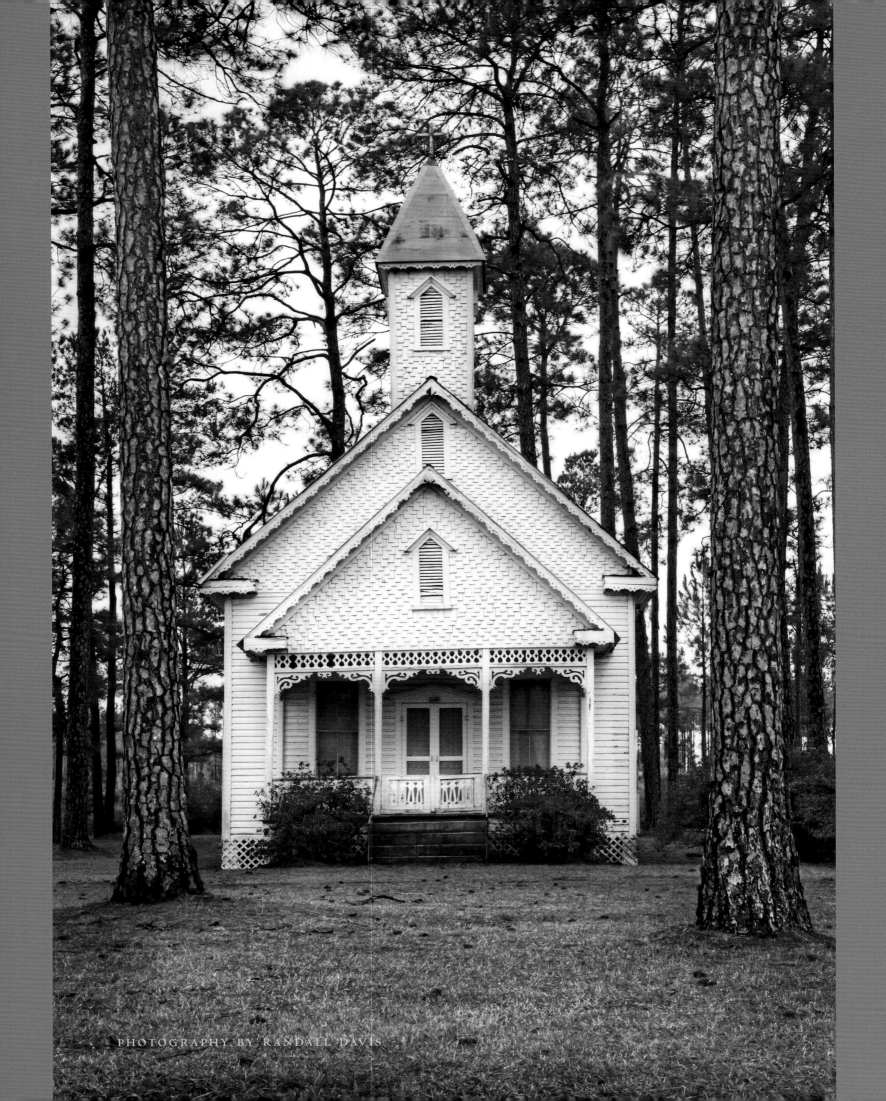

Old Ruskin

The exact dates of Old Ruskin Church organization and construction appear to be lost, but a sister church located nearby—Ezekiel New Congregational Methodist (see previous entry)—was built in 1899. Manning Thigpen was likely the builder responsible for both churches as the architecture and detailing of these Carpenter Gothic structures are strikingly similar. Although no known records indicate even its original name, we believe this church was built some years before Ezekiel, probably for a Methodist congregation, when the sawmill village here was known as Duke.

The Old Ruskin Church is all that is left of the town of Ruskin. The name was changed near the end of the nineteenth century from Duke to Ruskin in honor of John Ruskin, an English art patron and socialist who espoused and promoted a utopian society that, according to Wikipedia, would "show that contemporary life could still be enjoyed in the countryside, with land being farmed traditionally, with minimal mechanical assistance." Georgia's version of this Ruskinite colony was formed in 1898 by the American Settlers Association, a group of farmers looking to form a new community embracing Ruskin's social philosophy. They moved to Duke, changed its name to Ruskin, and bought 1,000 acres on which to settle.

Today it's not entirely clear how successful the colony became, how many people joined the effort, or whether they ever worshipped in the church. In any case, within just a few years the Ruskinites gave up, and the community was abandoned by 1901. Apart from this church that came to bear the name of Ruskin, nothing remains today of that utopian-minded community.

The Old Ruskin Church has remained active through the years. The current pastor, whose deep family ties in the area include a grandfather who helped in the construction of the church, has been at this pulpit since the 1950s. Maintenance and minimal modernization over the years keep Old Ruskin Church viable for a twenty-first-century rural congregation.

The curved ceiling raises the eye, imparting to the sanctuary a sense of openness. The columns that support the large steeple and belfry are less visually intrusive because of chamfering. The large windows on all four walls, assisted by the bright paint, provide abundant light within.

The fancy scrollwork and patterning of the altar rail echo the more elaborate Carpenter Gothic design elements of the exterior and make a strong design statement in this largely austere interior.

This ornate pulpit is a triumph of rural Carpenter Gothic ornamentation and design. The builder of the Ruskin church was a master craftsman with a strong sense of design.

This little church in the pines is a good example of loving care and faithful stewardship of one of the most unusual rural churches in the Georgia backcountry, preserving it for future generations.

Barnett Methodist

Barnett Methodist offers a wonderful example of the visual power of these old rural churches. It is also an uplifting example of how a church can be rescued from the brink of disaster by caring citizens of the community and saved for future generations to come.

The history of the town of Barnett is tied to the railroad. When tracks were being laid for the Georgia Railroad in the 1830s, rural towns and villages began to appear and disappear as a result. Barnett sprang up as a watering station and depot on the Augusta–Atlanta line. Being sited at the junction of the spur line to Washington, Georgia, completed in 1853, clinched Barnett's importance to the railroad. The railroad related infrastructure included a stone depot, a well, and an elevated watering tank for the steam engine. Around this railroad junction town emerged stores, offices, livery stables, a blacksmith, farriers, and homes. Beader Lawrence Battle Sr., a member of a prominent Warren County family, donated the land for the church and cemetery in 1876, and Barnett Methodist was constructed shortly thereafter.

The oldest documented graves in the cemetery are those of the benefactor's wife, Anna Proctor Battle (1840–1877), and of Battle himself (1829–1878). Battle's daughter Marye Lulu Battle, who died in 1900 at the age of thirty-five, is buried here and watched over by what some have called the Angel of Barnett, one of the most moving gravestones we have seen in Georgia.

The town's long decline began in the early twentieth century, as the railroad, the businesses, and the residents left one by one. The stone depot was torn down in the 1960s. In 2013, the Reverend Glen Hendley and his wife, Rachel, purchased the church property and set about its repair and restoration for the purpose of occasional services and other community events.

Before the private owners stepped in, the building was on the verge of total destruction, largely due to a failure of the composition shingle roof. The church at the center of this former railroad town was well on its way to the sad fate met by all of the town's other original structures.

Emptied of pews and nearly everything else, the sanctuary nonetheless reveals its origins as a postbellum rural Methodist church. The wood trim framing the apse opening is unexpectedly elegant and graceful. However, water damage from the leaking roof has caused much damage top to bottom.

As apparent here, the old roof had been compromised so as to
threaten the whole structure. In the foreground is the graceful
Angel of Barnett standing over Marye Lulu Battle's grave. The oldest
documented interment was in 1877, and the cemetery continued
to receive remains until at least 2005.

It is hard to believe that this recent photo of the rescued Barnett Methodist Church was taken only a year after the earlier photos. Only a photograph taken at Easter might be more appropriate to convey the rebirth that Barnett Methodist Church has experienced. A new roof and the dedicated commitment of the Hendleys made this remarkable transformation possible.

PHOTOGRAPHY BY GAIL DES JARDIN

Fountain Campground

This camp meeting ground developed as part of the Second Great Awakening that swept the new nation in the early nineteenth century. Also known as the Great Revival, this Protestant movement spread by means of circuit riders and established deep roots, especially in the South. As a result, Baptist, Presbyterian, and particularly Methodist congregations surged. Revivals in this period attracted large numbers of people and therefore took place outdoors at an encampment, initially in open spaces or in groves, thus the term "camp meeting." This phenomenon was widespread in Georgia and became so embedded in the state's religious tradition that some camp meeting places have survived into the twenty-first century and are still going strong.

One of the earliest to be established in Georgia, Fountain Campground is still thriving nearly two centuries after its founding. A board of trustees, constituted of members from the three counties in which the property lies, runs the facility. This includes a central tabernacle, around which have been built family-owned cabins, often referred to as tents.

We are indebted to the *New Georgia Encyclopedia* for its helpful information on camp-meeting grounds.

Revival campgrounds developed around a central structure where the meetings themselves took place. Many of the architectural characteristics of these central structures, sometimes called tabernacles and sometimes arbors, as described by the *New Georgia Encyclopedia*, are visible here. These include the "large square timber supports, angle braces, and exposed trusses topped by massive sheltering roofs." As in many of the other campgrounds across the state, Fountain's tabernacle is roofed with tin.

According to journalist Billy Hobbs, "people are said to have been coming to Fountain Campground as early as the late 1700s." Entire families traveled here in horse-drawn wagons "packed with enough food and other supplies to last for an entire week." They would set up camp, fanning out around the tabernacle. Camping in the same spot year after year, families hand down their sites from generation to generation, slowly improving on and adding to the "tent."

Power lines and a plastic child's picnic table signal the unmistakable introduction of modernity to this eighteenth-century religious tradition. The community-life emphasis conveyed by this outdoor seating, however, is firmly rooted in the spirit of Fountain Campground's origins.

This sign greets travelers along State Route 80 near the Warren-Wilkes County line. The scenery around Fountain hasn't changed much in two hundred years. The nearby river and creek still meander through relatively flat land, and the campground remains surrounded by a mixed pine and hardwood forest.

Crescent Hill Baptist

Crescent Hill Baptist is nestled in the North Georgia foothills overlooking the picturesque Nacoochee Valley, formed over thousands of years by the Chattahoochee River. The church also overlooks the site of a historically significant ancient mounded burial site of the Mississippian Indian peoples known as Mound Builders. The mound has been excavated several times, most recently in 1915 by archaeologists who removed the remains of seventy-five individuals. The high number of burials and other excavated evidence suggests that this area had been well populated and developed since about 1300. After the 1915 dig, a reconstruction of the mound was placed at the same location, now part of Hardman Farm State Historic Site.

The Cherokee land on which the church stands was purchased after the Treaty of 1819 by Daniel Brown, who then settled near here. Captain James H. Nichols of Milledgeville bought the property fifty years later in 1869. Nichols developed a number of buildings there, including the Victorian-style house on what is now Hardman Farm. Nichols was also responsible for the completion of the church in 1872, then known as the Nacoochee Presbyterian Church. It was one of the first churches in rural Georgia to adopt an emerging Victorian style now called Gothic Revival or Carpenter Gothic.

The farm property changed hands in 1893 and was resold a decade later to Dr. Lamartine Griffin Hardman, perhaps best known as a two-term governor of Georgia (1927–1931). The property remained in the Hardman family until 1999, when it was deeded over to the state of Georgia, which now operates it as a historic site.

By about 1903, the Nacoochee Presbyterian congregation moved to a new building, and the sanctuary remained unused until 1921, when Hardman allowed a group of Baptists to hold their services there. They renamed the church Crescent Hill Baptist. Some members of this still-active congregation are descended from the church founders. The main part of the church building has remained unchanged: the pulpit, pews, and stained glass are original. Crescent Hill is a remarkable rural church with uncommon architecture and charm.

The interior of the church reveals a radical departure from the simple rectangle many churches opened into. The detailed scroll work, applied ornamentation, fancifully formed and decorated support columns and trusses are eye-popping— even the wallboards have an inlaid lancet shape. The stained-glass frame behind the altar may originally have been a window to the outside, where there is now a small addition.

These windows are characteristic of the Carpenter Gothic style, with a twist. They are created by mounting a pair of large, pointed Gothic windows with clear glass panes that are laid within diagonal mullions. Those two large windows are then capped by a smaller, colored pane window placed on its point, cleverly creating another Gothic decorative element. This was unique church design for its era.

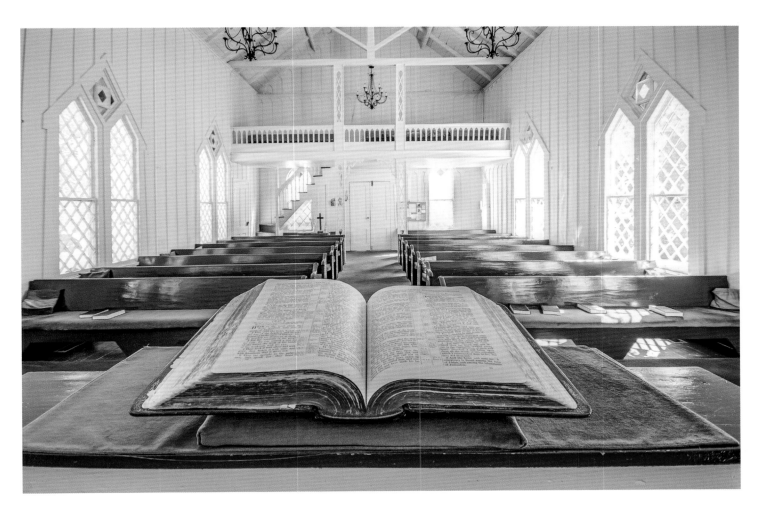

The builders of this church repeated the same Gothic lancet motif throughout the church. The diamond-lattice fretwork in the columns supporting the gallery echoes the diamond pattern in the windows. The exposed-beam construction raises the roof, so to speak, incorporating the arch detail.

The monochromatic white paint, exposed truss construction, and board-and-batten arched panels contribute to the ethereal atmosphere in this church.

The Indian Mound in front of the church was built many centuries ago by Mississippian Indian peoples who dwelled in this area of the south. Examination in the nineteenth century revealed that it, among other things, served as a crypt for seventy-five of these natives. The gazebo was constructed and placed on the mound top in the late 1800s by the landowner at that time, Captain James H. Nichols. Some refer to it as one of the most popular photo sites in Georgia. We can certainly see why that claim might be true.

Friendship Baptist

Records are scant, but we understand that Friendship Baptist was started by Clark's Station Baptist in January 1826 and that it was constituted on May 7, 1831, with thirty-three members, twelve of whom were black. The date of construction of this unassuming, gable-end church atop a gentle rise is unknown, although the oldest grave in the cemetery is from 1847. According to Robert Gardner's *History of the Georgia Baptist Association, 1784–1984*, the Friendship total membership was fifty in 1860, split almost evenly between white and black.

Despite the fact that Friendship Baptist has been inactive since about 1980, the building remains in surprisingly good shape, as evidenced by the little-used dirt track meandering up from Route 193 to the building. We were fortunate to have a local contact who arranged with the trustees managing the property for us to see the interior of the church. The trustees primarily oversee care of the cemetery and the exterior of the church. We are grateful for their stewardship of this rural jewel.

The church's location on a grassy rise allows light to flood in through the generous, clear-glass windows. The original heart-pine pews have developed a rich patina. Adding interest to an otherwise boxlike structure's interior is the simple but elegant trussed-rafter, cathedral ceiling. The ravages of time are revealed by the tie rod added sometime after construction to stabilize the structure and keep the walls from collapsing.

The wide wallboards and basic window framing form a backdrop for the modestly elegant pews, which feature subtle curves and fold-up kneelers. The proximity of the pews to the windows may entice the visitor to sit awhile to enjoy the view of the Georgia countryside.

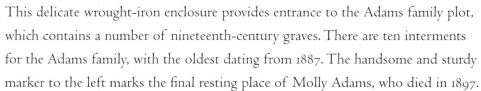

This delicate wrought-iron enclosure provides entrance to the Adams family plot, which contains a number of nineteenth-century graves. There are ten interments for the Adams family, with the oldest dating from 1887. The handsome and sturdy marker to the left marks the final resting place of Molly Adams, who died in 1897.

What makes Friendship Baptist Church somewhat distinct from other front-gable churches we have seen is its lack of a front porch, steeple, and apse. Typical of this style, however, is the diamond motif vent in the gable. The cemetery lies hard by the front entrance of the church. In the foreground are three traditional, nineteenth-century markers. The engraved, flush marble ledger marker in the center is flanked by two false crypts, one with brick sides and the other in marble.

Acknowledgments

The creation of *Historic Rural Churches of Georgia* has taken a number of years in terms of research, fieldwork, and recruiting and deploying photojournalists, among other tasks. Given the sheer number of people who have made valuable suggestions and contributions to this effort, it would be impossible for us to recognize all of them here. However, we do have a core of advisors, supporters, and friends to whom we are deeply grateful and who we feel must be acknowledged. Our volunteer photographers were so essential to these efforts that we chose to dedicate the book to them and to include a personal biographical sketch of each.

Early on, we reached out to a cadre of experts and advisors for technical advice, historical content, and general counsel. Among those were Charles Jones, Georgia Baptist Convention historian; Terry Fleming, Augusta District, NGA Methodist Conference; Deborah Madera, Pitts Theological Library, Emory; Teya Ryan, president, and Mike McDougald, chairman, Georgia Public Broadcasting; Dan Roper, publisher, *Georgia Backroads Magazine*; Todd Groce, president, Georgia Historical Society; Laura Hardman and Steve Hochman, the Carter Center; Jamil Zainaldin, president, Georgia Humanities Council; Carole Moore, DNR Historical Preservation; Kevin Davis, Wilkerson Construction; Kate Willis, Swamp Gravy; and Tommy Herrington, Gay Construction Company. Our early local field scouts and advisors were Joel McCray, Greene County; Sistie Hudson, Hancock County; Betty Slaton, Wilkes County; Carol Faz, Oglethorpe County; Bobby Jones, Taliaferro County; and Glenn and Rachel Hendley, Warren County.

Since we have had no formal organization, employees, or money, we have relied from the beginning on the kindness of friends and strangers who volunteered to help and donated their labor for free, and we are forever grateful. Our corporate board consists of Tom Gay, Gay Construction; Scott Ward, principal; Warner Summers; and Tom Beard, Morgan Stanley. Our technical gurus, Kevin Guebert, Jay Schneider, and Richard Ortiz, have provided website assistance. Brad McColl has been very helpful with our video efforts, along with Jonathan Wickham. One cannot start a nonprofit enterprise without legal help, and we have had the best possible from Ed Dobbs, Tommy Thompson, and Lauren Jirak at Parker, Hudson, Rainer, and Dobbs; Peter Smith at Thompson Hine; and Randy Smith at RealCorp Legal.

Finally, our collegial relationship with managers and staff at the University of Georgia Libraries and the University of Georgia Press was invaluable to our successful completion of this project. Without their forgiving and agreeable support, two neophyte authors and editors like us would have been doomed to fail. Thank you, Toby Graham, head of the University of Georgia Libraries, and Chantel Dunham, director of development. At UGA Press we were ably supported and encouraged by Lisa Bayer, director; Elizabeth Crowley, editorial assistant; Jon Davies, assistant director for editorial, design, and production; Melissa Bugbee Buchanan, assistant editorial, design, and production manager; Erin New, designer/art director; and Deborah Oliver, our copy editor, who kept us in line during that exhaustive process.

Many thanks to all.

SONNY SEALS & GEORGE S. HART

Selected Bibliography

BOOKS

Amor, E. H. *The Cemeteries of Greene County, Georgia.* Athens, Ga.: Agee
    Publishers, 1987.

Asbury, Francis. *Journal of Rev. Francis Asbury: Bishop of the Methodist
    Episcopal Church.* 3 vols. New York: Lane & Scott, 1852. Accessed at
    http://books.google.com.

Bell, Malcolm, Jr. *Major Butler's Legacy: Five Generations of a Slaveholding
    Family.* Athens: University of Georgia Press, 1987.

Bonner, John C. *A History of Georgia Agriculture: 1732–1860.* Athens:
    University of Georgia Press, 1964.

Bryant, Jonathan M. *How Curious a Land: Conflict and Change in Greene
    County, Georgia, 1850–1885.* Chapel Hill: University of North
    Carolina Press, 1996.

Cole, Mildred Jackson, and Mt. Enon Historical Committee.
    *From Stage Coaches to Train Whistles: History of Gum Pond, Mt. Enon, Baconton
    in Mitchell County, Georgia; 1856–1976; Including Biographical Sketches and
    Genealogies of Pioneer Families.* [Baconton, Ga.]: Mt. Enon Historical
    Committee, [1977].

Crowley, John G. *Primitive Baptists of the Wiregrass South: 1815 to the Present.*
    Gainesville: University Press of Florida, 2013.

Gardner, Robert G. *A History of the Georgia Baptist Association, 1784–1984.*
    Atlanta: Georgia Baptist Historical Society, 1988.

Gourley, Bruce Thomas. *Baptists in Middle Georgia during the Civil War.*
    Macon, Ga.: Mercer University Press, 2011.

Harden, William. *A History of Savannah and South Georgia.* Vol. 2. Chicago:
    Lewis Publishing Co., 1913. Accessed at http://files.usgwarchives
    .net/ga/chatham/bios/gbs527flannery.txt.

Hemperley, Marion R. *Historic Indian Trails of Georgia.* Athens: Garden
    Club of Georgia, 1989.

History of the Baptist Denomination in Georgia. Atlanta, Ga.: Jas. P. Harrison
    & Co., 1881.

*History of the South Georgia Conference: The United Methodist Church, 1866–1984:
    With Historical Sketches of the 713 Active Churches.* [St. Simons Island, Ga.?]:
    South Georgia Conference Commission on Archives and History for
    the Bicentennial of American Methodism, 1984.

History of Warren County. Warrenton, Ga.: Warren County Chamber of
    Commerce, n.d.

Inscoe, John C. *The Civil War in Georgia: A New Georgia Encyclopedia
    Companion.* Athens: University of Georgia Press, 2011.

Johnston, Richard M. *Dukesborough Tales: The Chronicles of Mr. Bill Williams.*
    Upper Saddle Creek, N.J.: Gregg Press, 1968.

Jones, George Wimberly. *Observations on Dr. Stevens's History of Georgia.*
    London: Forgotten Books, 2013 [1849].

Keister, Douglas, *Stories in Stone: A Field Guide to Cemetery Symbolism and
    Iconography.* Layton, Utah: Gibbs Smith, 2004.

Kilde, Jeanne Halgren. *When Church Became Theatre: The Transformation of
    Evangelical Architecture and Worship in Nineteenth-Century America.* New York:
    Oxford University Press, 2002.

Knight, E. V. *The Baptist Church of Christ at Ramoth: A Short History for Years
    1836–1900.* N.p.: E. V. Knight, 1997.

Leslie, Kent Anderson. *Woman of Color, Daughter of Privilege: Amanda America
    Dickson, 1849–1893.* Athens: University of Georgia Press, 1996.

McWhirter, Cameron. *Red Summer: The Summer of 1919 and the Awakening of
    Black America.* New York: Henry Holt, 2011.

Meyer, Richard, ed. *Cemeteries and Gravemarkers: Voices of American Culture.*
    Logan: Utah State University Press, 1992.

Miller, Alexander Lee. *History of Bethel Association Including Centennial
    Meeting: Centennial Meeting Held with Baptist Church at Edison, Georgia, October
    25, 26, 27, 1932.* A. L. Miller, Edison, Ga., Moderator. W. H. Joyner,
    Coleman, Ga., Clerk. Compiled and edited by Alexander Lee Miller,
    Moderator of Association, 1909–34. [Edison, Ga.: N.p., 1934?].
    Accessed at http://files.usgwarchives.net/ga/randolph/churches
    /nbb36benevole.txt.

Morton, William J. *The Story of Georgia's Boundaries: A Meeting of History and Geography.* Atlanta: Georgia History Press, 2009.

Raper, Arthur F. *Tenants of the Almighty.* London: Macmillan, 1943.

Robinson, R. L. *History of the Georgia Baptist Association.* [Atlanta]: N.p., 1928.

Rozier, John. *The Houses of Hancock, 1785–1865.* Decatur, Ga.: Auldfarran Books, 1999.

Smith, George G. *The Story of Georgia and the Georgia People.* Macon, Ga.: George G. Smith Publishers, 1900.

Smith, George Gillman. *The History of Methodism in Georgia and Florida: From 1785 to 1865.* Macon, Ga.: J. W. Burke & Co., 1877.

Stevens, William Bacon. *A History of Georgia.* New York: D. Appleton & Co., 1847.

Wetherington, Mark V. *The New South Comes to Wiregrass Georgia, 1860–1910.* Knoxville: University of Tennessee Press, 1994.

Williams, Carolyn White. *History of Jones County, Georgia, for One Hundred Years, Specifically 1807–1907.* Macon, Ga.: J. W. Burke Co., 1957.

Williams, David S. *From Mounds to Megachurches: Georgia's Religious Heritage.* Athens: University of Georgia Press, 2008.

ARCHIVES IN GEORGIA

Georgia Baptist Convention Historical Archive and Museum, Atlanta.

Georgia Baptist History Repository, Jack Tarver Library, Mercer University, Macon.

UMC North Georgia Conference Archives, Pitts Theology Library, Emory University, Atlanta.

UMC South Georgia Conference Archives, Arthur J. Moore Methodist Museum and Library, St. Simons Island.

PAMPHLETS, PRINT ARTICLES, AND WEB

Augusta Chronicle. http://beta.mirror.augusta.com/.

Bark Camp Church. "Detailed History." Bark Camp Church, Midville. www.barkcampchurch.org/detailed-history.html.

"A Brief History of Thyatira Presbyterian Church: 1796–1951." Jackson County Historical Society, HS-87.12.104.

Brown's Guide to Georgia. Peachtree City, Georgia. www.brownsguides.com.

Butler, Sherri. Article in *Fitzgerald Herald-Leader,* 16 August 1995. Accessed at www.facebook.com/saveyoungschapel.

"Camp-Meeting Grounds." *New Georgia Encyclopedia.* 20 November 2013. www.georgiaencyclopedia.org/articles/arts-culture/camp-meeting-grounds.

Cooksey, Elizabeth B. "St. Marys." *New Georgia Encyclopedia.* 24 September 2014. www.georgiaencyclopedia.org/articles/counties-cities-neighborhoods/st-marys.

Derden, John K. "Bark Camp Baptist Church." Undated. www.barkcampchurch.org/detailed-history.html.

Episcopal Community of McIntosh County. "Saint Andrew's and Saint Cyprians's [*sic*] Churches: About Us." http://StAndrewsStCyprians.GeorgiaEpiscopal.org/?page_id=19.

"Fields Chapel History." Fields Chapel United Methodist Church. Canton: n.d. http://fieldschapel.org/our-church/fields-chapel-history.

Forte, Suzanne, transcriber. "Church History of Providence Baptist Church, Shady Dale, Jasper County, Georgia." Providence Baptist Church, 2005. www.rootsweb.ancestry.com/~gajasper/excerptsprovidence.htm.

"Fountain Campground Plays Host to Annual Campmeeting Starting Saturday." *McDuffie Mirror,* July 24, 2015. http://mirror.augusta.com/stories/060205/com_fountain.shtml.

Friends of Cemeteries of Middle Georgia. http://friendsofcems.org/.

Galileo. www.galileo.usg.edu/?Welcome.

Gardner, Robert G. "Georgia Baptist Church Records Located in the Georgia Baptist History Depository, Special Collections, Jack Tarver Library, Mercer University, Macon, Georgia." Georgia Baptist Church Records, Special Collections, Jack Tarver Library, Mercer University, Macon. Updated January 3, 2012.

Georgia Trust for Historic Preservation. www.georgiatrust.org.

"Historical Atlases and Maps of U.S. and States." *MapofUS.org.* www.mapofus.org/.

"Historical Maps." Hargrett Rare Book and Manuscript Library, University of Georgia, Athens. www.libs.uga.edu/hargrett/maps/.

"Historic Buildings: Nichols-Hunnicutt-Hardman House and Farm." Sautee Nacoochee Center. www.snca.org/snc/museums/history/homes/bldgHardman.php.

"Historic [Van Wert] Church Has Unique Past; Worship Centers, Civil War and Famed Evangelist." *Polk County Standard Journal,* August 6, 2015. Accessed at www.northwestgeorgianews.com/polkfishwrap/news/local/historic-church-has-unique-past-worship-centers-civil-war-and/article_4bb2ea6e-3c3f-11e5-88dd-433760742f42.html.

A History of Cove United Methodist Church. Foreword by Pastor Read Williamson. [Chickamauga, Ga.: Cove United Methodist Church] September 1975, 15 pp.

"History of the Powelton, Ga. Methodist Church. Mayfield Charge. Agusta [*sic*] District." [1951] 1971 Augusta Dist., no. 120. Pitts Theology Library, Emory University, Atlanta.

Hobbs, Billy W. "Christian Tradition: Families Flock to Fountain Campground for Worship." *McDuffie Mirror,* July 24, 2015. Accessed at http://mirror.augusta.com/stories/061407/new_132288.shtml.

Hurst, Robert Latimer. "Much History in Abandoned Ezekiel Church." *Waycross (Georgia) Journal-Herald,* April 25, 2003, P-8.

Huxford, Folks. "Liberty Baptist Church History." In *The History of Brooks County, Georgia, 1858–1948.* Athens: n.p., 1949.

"Index of /ga/banks/military/civilwar." USGW Archives. http://files.usgwarchives.net/ga/banks/military/civilwar/.

"Jerusalem Church." *Georgia Salzburger Society.* http://georgiasalzburgers .com/jerusalem-church.htm.

Jones, Mary Calloway. *Mercer at Penfield: 1833–1871: Centennial Celebration.* 2nd ed. May 27, 1933. 20 pp. Accessed at http://libraries.mercer .edu/repository/bitstream/handle/10898/2851/Penfield%20 Booklet.pdf?sequence=1.

Kilpatrick, W. L. *The Hephzibah Baptist Association Centennial, from 1794 to 1894.* Accessed at http://baptisthistoryhomepage.com /ga.hephzibah.assoc.hist.html.

Lawson, Harrell. *History of St. Paul CME Church: Organized 1857; Property Deeded 1870–1877.* 2005. Accessed at http://www.georgiagenealogy .org/hancock2/stpaulcme.html.

McWhiter, Cameron. "The Spiritual Ground of History." *Harvard Divinity Bulletin* 39, nos. 3–4 (2011). Accessed at www.hds .harvard.edu/news-events/harvard-divinity-bulletin/articles /the-spiritual-ground-of-history.

New Georgia Encyclopedia. University of Georgia Press and Georgia Humanities Council. www.georgiaencyclopedia.org/.

Noegel, Richard. *A History of Bethesda Baptist Church: Union Point, Georgia 30669.* Undated. Accessed at http://bethesda1.homestead.com /history.html.

"Our Georgia History." *Our Georgia History.* http://www.ourgeorgiahistory .com/.

Plains Baptist Church. [Plains, Ga.] 4 pp. Undated.

"Restoration Work Continues on Historic Van Wert Church." *Polk County Standard Journal,* May 22, 2015. Accessed at www.northwestgeorgianews.com/polkfishwrap/news/local /restoration-work-continues-on-historic-van-wert-church /article_8cffeb4e-008e-11e5-a33a-b337435c7d9b.html.

RootsWeb.com. http://rootsweb.ancestry.com/.

"Taliaferro County History—Taliaferro County Historical Society." USGenWeb Archives. http://files.usgwarchives.net/ga/taliaferro /history/tchsfiles.txt.

Toney, Charles G. *Hebron Presbyterian Church: God's Pilgrim People 1796– 1996.* Chairman Roy Winchester Coker. Banks County, Ga.: Hebron Historical Society, 1995.

Van Wert Baptist Church. *The Church Book of the Baptist Church at Van Wert, Paulding County, Georgia.* Minutes 1842–1849. File transcribed by Cassandra Robertson Newby, April 6, 2010. Accessed at www.usgennet.org/usa/ga/county/paulding1/church/VanWert .02.html.

Wikipedia. Wikimedia Foundation. www.wikipedia.org/.

About the Photographers

In addition to being talented photographers, these volunteers are passionate advocates for the rural churches and skilled researchers who are a vital part of the process. Many times the history of the old churches is available only in obscure places and local sources. Much of the discovery, research, and documentation is done in the field by this dedicated group.

RANDY CLEGG

Photographs of Hebron Presbyterian, Mt. Olivet Methodist, Carroll's Methodist, Grace-Calvary Episcopal, and Crescent Hill Baptist

An amateur photographer from Buford, Georgia, I began to learn the craft and to be intentional with the photos I take after purchasing my first digital SLR camera in 2007. To learn photography I studied beautiful photos, and those on the Historic Rural Churches of Georgia (HRCGA) website made me want to contribute to these efforts.

RANDALL DAVIS

Photographs of High Bluff Primitive Baptist, Ezekiel New Congregational Methodist, and Old Ruskin

A freelance photographer now residing in Statesboro, Georgia, I took up photography after working as a land surveyor and as a cabinet and furniture maker. I also served a tour as a platoon leader in the army and worked as a research biologist in fisheries for the Alaska Department of Fish and Game. My interest in history and preservation of significant structures brought me to HRCGA, especially the documentation aspect of their goals.

GAIL DES JARDIN

Photographs of Alpine Presbyterian, Sardis Presbyterian, Penfield Baptist, Wrightsboro Methodist, Cove Methodist, and Fountain Campground

In 1992, I was neck-deep in listening to R.E.M. and following the interests of lead singer Michael Stipe, whose photography hobby piqued my interest. As a child, we lived next to the only cemetery in town, and I grew up fascinated by its character and mystery. This fascination with churches and cemeteries has stayed with me, and photography has become a natural avenue for paying reverence to these spiritual gathering places.

SCOTT FARRAR

Photographs of Young's Chapel Methodist, Powelton Baptist, Powelton Methodist, St. Paul CME, Concord Primitive Baptist, Clinton Methodist, Antioch Baptist (Taliaferro County), Locust Grove Catholic, and Barnett Methodist

A native Georgian, I reside in Atlanta. I am a hobbyist photographer with an emphasis on historical and architectural photography. In the HRCGA project I can combine three of my passions: photography, exploring, and history. I love traveling the back roads of Georgia and the South to find places and stories long forgotten, with the hopes of making their legends and beauty known to future generations.

JOHN KIRKLAND

Photographs of Bark Camp Baptist, Kiokee Baptist, Jerusalem Lutheran, Big Buckhead Baptist, and Carswell Grove Baptist

I am a photographer living in Augusta, Georgia, on the banks of the Savannah River. Photography for me started out as a necessity to capture memories of my children, but it has become a passion—maybe even an obsession. Since here in Augusta we are surrounded by many old towns, churches, and architecture, all set in the charm of the classic South, much of my photography focuses on the historical.

SCOTT MacINNIS

Photographs of Fields Chapel United Methodist, Bethesda Baptist, Apple Valley Baptist, Thyatira Presbyterian, Beth Salem Presbyterian, Philomath Presbyterian, Van Wert Methodist, and Friendship Baptist

I am a nature and fine-art photographer living in Johns Creek, Georgia. Although I've lived all over the United States, I now consider myself a fully converted transplant. I fell in love with the rural South, and I have been photographing Georgia back roads for years. I'm thrilled to be part of a group helping to document and preserve these rural beauties from the past.

WAYNE MOORE

Photographs of First Presbyterian of St. Marys, Midway Congregational, Sapelo First African Baptist, and St. Cyprian's Episcopal

An early interest in photography led me to pursue a bachelor's degree in photography from the Savannah College of Art and Design. My company, Back River Photography LLC, allows me to live out my passion of photographing the Low Country and its people. The history and architecture—particularly of old churches—of Georgia's coastal region inspire me.

STEVE ROBINSON

Photographs of Liberty Baptist, Bethlehem Primitive Baptist, Mt. Enon Baptist, Benevolence Baptist, Antioch Primitive Baptist (Stewart County), Plains Baptist, and St. Mark's Lutheran

From Leesburg, Georgia, I am a husband, father, grandfather, and amateur photographer. For years I have enjoyed exploring and photographing the rural areas of South Georgia. Small country churches have always been a vital part of the rural Georgia landscape and were once the center of life for the communities they anchored. I attempt to document their simple beauty in order to help tell their stories.